MORE Fun with Split Ring Tatting

Karen Bovard © 2013

Published by: The ShuttleSmith Publishing Company
9102 Poppleton Avenue
Omaha, Nebraska 68124

TheShuttleSmith@gmail.com

ISBN: 978-0-9835441-1-1

© Karen Bovard 2013 All Rights Reserved

CONTENTS

Introduction to Split Ring Tatting Visual Patterns/Enhancement Suggestions	pages 2 to 9
Herringbone/Chevron/Heart Designs	pages 10 to 13
Celtic Inspired Designs	pages 14 to 23
Tessellation/Lace-Tessellation Inspired Designs	pages 24 to 55
Split Ring & Take-Off Ring creation by Needle Tatting Technique	pages 56 to 63

    The creation of this book started when I realized that I could recreate, in tatting, the 'houndstooth' pattern of my pants (probably 20 years ago). This started me on a wonderful learning/exploratory journey that let my creativity remain active even when I wasn't physically tatting. I discovered many repetitve-design ideas in clothing, accessories, flooring, architecture, etc. In actively searching the internet for more design ideas for my tatting projects, I learned that there is a name for these patterns: _Tessellation_. *Here is your free math lesson*: "A tessellation is created when a shape is repeated over and over again covering a plane without any gaps or overlaps. Another word for a tessellation is _tiling_. A brick wall is an example of tessellation." *(End official math lesson.)* However, in the definition of tessellation, there are 'no gaps or overlaps' in the formation of a pattern. This is contrary to lacemaking, where we have spaces ('negative space') of 'air/nothing' with thread around them to make a 'lacy' appearance. Some of the Split Ring Tatting designs in this book are True Tessellations (example: page 31) . However, the basic design elements have been manipulated to create 'Lace-Tessellations'---possibly a new art form (example: bottom-page 27). All my Lace-Tessellation & True-Tessellation inspired designs start with what I call 'Basic Design Elements'. These repetitve design patterns allow other design manipulations to create bookmark, edging, and cross patterns. *This book does not contain all my Tessellation inspired designs.....look for more in future books!*

    This book is also about COLOR. It utilizes more than one color of thread in a design, encouraging the tatter to go beyond monochromatic. Since many of the designs feature repetitive motifs, there are a lot of color variations possible. A word of caution: when you are using different thread colors in one piece, make sure that both threads are from the same manufacturer to ensure that the size between motifs is consistent. You may also see a slight difference in size of thread between different colors of the same manufacturer. This is probably due to the different dyeing processes of the different colors.

    All the designs are created entirely of Rings, either regular or split rings. No tatted chains are used. If you like the looks of these designs and want to have "MORE Fun with Split Rings", check out *Fun with Split Ring Tatting* (ISBN: 978-0-9835441-0-4, 2012)--it features 55 geometric designs and includes a more comprehensive introduction to Split Ring Tatting Technique.

> Special Thanks to Jennifer Bartling--my friend, editor.

No part of this book's patterns may be photocopied, mechanically or electronically transmitted without the author's written permission. *In other words, please respect the time and talent of the author to not reproduce this book.*

Guide/Key to Split Ring Visual Patterns

The following standard abbreviations are used

R   Ring

SR   Split Ring

TOR   Take Off Ring/Thrown Off Ring

▬   Picots

✚   Joins

> As in all Visual/Illustrated Patterns:
> - The first ring tatted that has a picot is when you will tat that picot.
> - The ensuing ring tatted that is associated with that same picot will be a join.

Key Points of Illustrated Patterns

<u>Color of Portions/Segments</u>
- each color represents one of two shuttle/thread sources

<u>Direction of the arcs (from dot to arrowheads)</u>
- shows which way regular rings and the portions of split rings are worked.
- gives direction to how the ring is to be tatted if Frontside/Backside Tatting technique is used.
- gives direction as to when the work is to be reversed.

<u>Colored Letters</u>
- dictate which portion of a split ring is to be tatted first ('A') with regular, transferred double stitches and then the ('B') portion with untransferred, reverse-stitch double stitches.
- if a split ring does not have a join or a TOR associated with it, the portions of the split ring can be tatted in any order (colored letters will not be indicated in this split ring).

<u>Numbered Rings</u>
All the rings (regular, take-off, or split ring) are numbered sequentially. Thus the path that the pattern is to be worked is to start at 'R1' and work in ascending order.

Path of the Pattern

How the pattern is worked (or the 'Path' of how the pattern is worked) is designated in Visual Patterns by the number inside the rings, next to either **R**, **SR**, or **TOR**.

Start at R1 and then progress numerically (1 then 2, then 3, then 4.....) through the pattern.

There are different ways or paths to take to tat the pattern other than the one that has been illustrated. However, the patterns have been carefully designed and charted to lessen the complexity of the pattern and to allow for the following conditions:
- The pattern can be worked continuously, from start to end in one round (or as few rounds as possible).
- Regular joins (not Split Ring Joining technique) can be used.
    - Regular joins must be made on the first portion of the split ring (the regular, transferred double stitches).
- Take off rings (TOR's) can be created without the need for an additional thread source.
    - TOR's are created (with only two shuttles/thread sources used) on the second portion of the split ring (the untransferred, reverse-stitch double stitches).
    - TOR's (which are regular rings) allow regular joins to be used.
- Regular rings are used as often as possible.

Regularly Tatted Rings as seen in Visual Patterns--Including Take Off Rings

- The <u>dot</u> is used to designate the starting point of the ring.

- The <u>arrowhead</u> designates the ending point of the ring.

'**R**' is used to designate a (regular) ring.

The larger '#'/'number' (after the 'R') designates the order in which the rings are tatted and thus how the pattern is worked.

As in other visual/diagrammed patterns, the '#' on the inside of the arc is the number of double stitches in that particular portion of the split ring and/or between picots and joins.

<u>A regular-tatted ring in Visual Pattern style is distinguished by the fact that</u>:
     -There is only one arc.
     -There is only one color used for the arc, starting dot and ending arrowhead.
     -The starting point and the ending point are at the same place on the ring.

Split Rings in Visual Patterns

Two <u>dots</u> of different colors are used to designate the starting points of the two different thread sources of a split ring. Each thread source has its own starting-point dot for every ring or split ring.

Two <u>arrowheads</u> are used to designate the ending points of the two thread sources of a split ring. Each thread source has it own ending-point arrowhead for every ring or split ring.

The <u>arcs</u> represent the different thread sources of the split ring. When you see a ring diagram with two colors in it, you know that it is a split ring.

The abbreviations '**SR**' are used. The '**S**' meaning 'Split' and the '**R**' meaning 'Ring'.

The larger '#'/'number' (after 'SR') designates the order in which the rings are tatted and thus how the pattern is worked.

As in other visual/diagrammed patterns, the number on the inside of the arc is the number of double stitches in that particular portion of the split ring and/or picots and joins.

When all the illustrations are put into one diagram, the complete path of where the split ring is started, where it ends, the direction that the portions of the split rings are made, and stitch counts of the portions of the split ring designate the attributes of the split ring.

Numbered Rings in Visual Patterns

How the pattern is worked (or the 'Path' of how the pattern is worked) is designated in Visual Patterns by the number inside the rings, next to either **R**, **SR**, or **TOR**.

Start at R1 and then progress numerically (1 then 2, then 3, then 4.....) through the pattern.

COLORED LETTERS IN VISUAL PATTERNS

Some of the split rings in the visual patterns will have colored letter designations *(inside the ring, and next to the stitch count)* and some will not.

If a split ring does not have a join or a Take Off Ring associated with it, the portions of the split ring can be tatted in any order.

ILLUS A is a split ring that can be tatted in one of two ways--either choice appropriate:
   A. The 12-stitch (red) portion can be tatted first with regular, transferred stitches and then the 4-stitch (green) portion is tatted with reverse, untransferred stitches. **OR**
   B. Tat the 4-stitch (green) portion first with regular, transferred stitches and then the 12-stitch (red) portion is tatted with reverse, untransferred stitches.

However, the order in which the split ring portions are tatted in some split rings is important for two reasons:
   1. To easily create *joins* utilizing traditional tatting joining techinque--NOT split ring joining tatting *(which is more cumbersome to master and doesn't create as visually-effective a join)*.
      --Done from the *first portion* (the regular, transferred double stitches) of the split ring.
   2. To effect the creation of *Take-Off Rings (TOR's)* without the need to use a third thread source.
      --Done from the *second portion* (the reverse, untransferred double stitches) of the split ring.

The presence of colored letters in *ILLUS B* dictates that the 12-stitch (red) portion is to be tatted first with regular, transferred stitches and then the 4-stitch (green) portion is tatted second with reverse, untransferred stitches. Just like in the alphabet, 'A' comes before 'B' and thus the 'A' portion is done first.

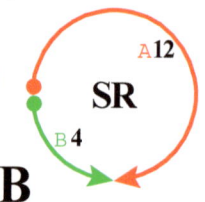

DIRECTION OF ARCS

The direction in which the arc is illustrated will give you clues as to:
   A. If the ring/split ring is to be tatted as a 'Frontside' or a 'Backside' element.
   B. When you need to Reverse or Turn the work (traditional written directions use 'RW' or 'T').

VISUAL PATTERN CLUES AS TO USE OF FRONTSIDE/BACKSIDE TATTING

The direction of the arc (as evidenced by the arrowhead) shows the direction that the ring is worked.

Traditionally tatted regular rings are tatted in a 'clockwise' direction.

If the arc of a regular ring is *'clockwise'* then the ring is tatted as a *'frontside'* ring. **ILLUS C**

If the arc of a regular ring is *'counter-clockwise'* then the ring is tatted as a *'backside'* ring. **ILLUS D**

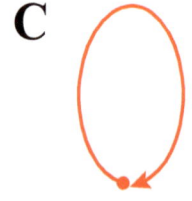

CLOCKWISE
Direction of Work
'Frontside' Ring
DS = Under then
Over Stitch

COUNTER-CLOCKWISE
Direction of Work
'Backside' Ring
DS = Over then
Under Stitch

Visual Pattern Clues as to use of Frontside/Backside Tatting (continued)

However, in split rings, both clockwise and counter-clockwise arcs/portions are part of each split ring. The direction of the first portion of the split ring made dictates whether the split ring is tatted as either a 'frontside' or a 'backside' ring.

ILLUS E is a 'Frontside' split ring because Portion A is 'clockwise'.

ILLUS F is a 'Backside' split ring because Portion A is 'counter-clockwise'.

E	CLOCKWISE First = 'Frontside' Ring	F	COUNTER-CLOCKWISE First = 'Backside' Ring
	With the 'Red' Shuttle make 12 regular, transferred double stitches: ***Under stitch-first; followed by Over Stitch***.		With the 'Red' Shuttle make 12 regular, transferred double stitches: ***Over Stitch-first; followed by Under Stitch***.
With 'Green' Shuttle make 4 reverse, untranferred double stitches: ***Over Stitch-First; followed by Under Stitch***.		With 'Green' Shuttle make 4 reverse, untranferred double stitches: ***Under Stitch-First; followed by Over Stitch***.	

If the split ring is not designated as to which portion is made first, it is up to the tatter to decide which portion to work first then second and thus, whether the split ring is either a 'frontside' or a 'backside' ring.

Visual Pattern Clues as to When to Reverse Work

If you tat one ring as a 'frontside' element (the first portion of a split ring &/or the regular ring is a clock-wise arc) and then the second ring is a 'backside' element (the first portion of a split ring &/or the regular ring is a counter-clockwise arrow) you will need to Reverse Work between these two rings. ***ILLUS G***

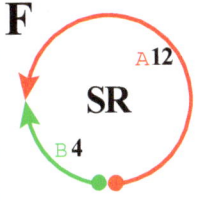

Closing Rings to Achieve a Round Shape

A round-shaped ring is achieved in two steps
1. Close the ring as in ***ILLUS H*** by pulling the working shuttle/thread downward, away from the base of the ring.
2. Use your fingers to push the ring into a round shape by pushing the ring in the direction of the arrows in ***ILLUS I***.

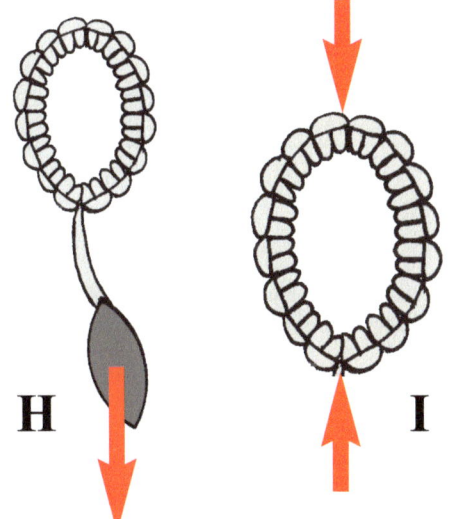

One may be tempted to close a ring by pulling the shuttle/thread toward the side of the ring while closing the ring. ***ILLUS J*** This will erroneously produce a misshapen ring due to the fact that the last double stitch-made will not align with the first double stitch-made. ***Black Arrow in ILLUS J***

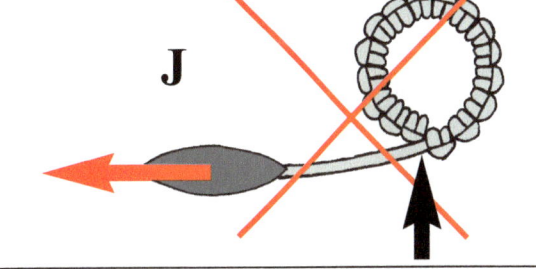

All the rings in this book are designed to be round-shaped.

ALL RINGS ARE TATTED WITH NO-SPACE OF THREAD BETWEEN RINGS

The visual effect of the pieces in this book is that each ring is closely adjacent to its neighboring ring(s). **ILLUS A**

In the same way that Joining Picots are used to simulate no space of thread between rings, all rings are started as close to one another as possible.

The challenge is to tat a piece so that an observer is unaware of the path of construction of the piece.

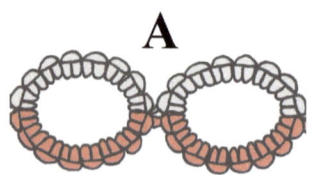

PICOT SIZE--USE OF JOINING PICOTS

The picots used in this book are all examples of Joining Picots. The pieces were designed with the idea that all the rings lie in close relationship with one another.

Joining picots are minute picots that barely allow for insertion of a tiny crochet hook. They are used only for joining, not as ornamental picots. A Joining Picot is barely recognizable as a picot loop. **ILLUS B**

A space of thread between the two double stitches that is creating the properly-sized Joining Picot is equal to one double stitch width. **ILLUS C**

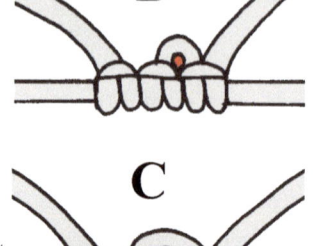

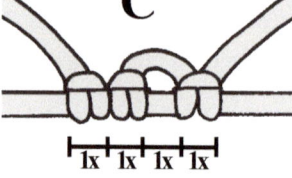

JOINING TOOLS

In the process of facilitating very tight joins between rings, very small joining picots are created. A small-gauge crochet hook is necessary to facilitate these joins.
  Crochet hook range: Size 8 to 14.
    (14 is the smallest).

Proper Joining Picot size is actually so small that at times it maybe dificult to get even a tiny crochet hook into the picot loop to use it. At these times, a dental-pick tool or a blunt-tipped sewing needle (such as a Tapestry needle--ca. Size 20, 22, or 24--*larger # equals smaller needle*) is handy to use to pull the picots out to a sufficient size to be able to easily insert a hook into to use as a join.

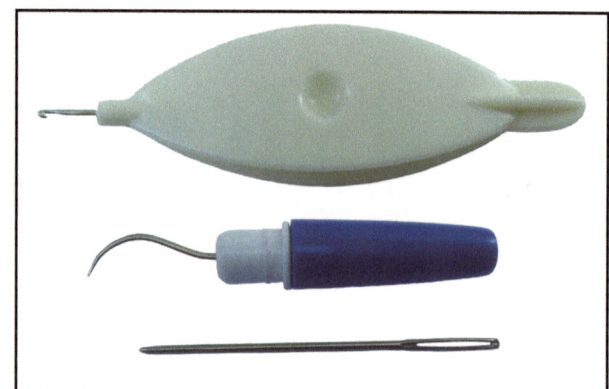

Author's Favorite Split Ring Tatting Tools

FORGOTTEN JOINING PICOT?

Not all hope is lost! Just insert your crochet hook or pick/needle between the stitches where the picot should be. Pull out this horizontal space of thread and use it as a picot. Picots formed this way will be an appropriate size for joining the patterns tatted with Split Ring Tatting technique in this book.

You can also add on to a previously-made piece, making it longer/larger by pulling out joining picots from between stitches.

USE OF FRONTSIDE/BACKSIDE TATTING & JOINING TECHNIQUE STRATEGIES

Frontside/Backside Tatting Technique is the formation of the Half/Double Stitches, Elements (Rings and Chains), and Joins in such a way that the 'reversed elements' would have the same appearance as the 'unreversed elements'. One side of the piece would have a 'frontside' appearance and the other side of the piece, a 'backside' appearance. This has also been known as 'Directional Tatting'. The name of 'Rightside/Wrongside Tatting' should not be used...there is a fair amount of aversion to this name by the tatting community. It is thought that there is no 'wrong' side to tatted lace.

There are two areas of tatting that will show if Frontside/Backside Tatting Technique has been used:
1. The double stitch formation process - most visible at the picots.
2. Joins.

NOTE: Frontside/Backside Tatting Technique is a tatting 'strategy'. It is not a required technique, but is an optional approach. Use (or nonuse) of Frontside/Backside Tatting is a personal choice.

However, due to the fact that many of the patterns in this book join different colored motifs together to create the design effect, this may suggest a further review of use of **Frontside/Backside Joining Technique**.

The act of making a regular *(sliding, not locking)* join adds an extra horizontal thread to the stitches being tatted. This horizontal thread is supplied by the picot you are joining to. This horizontal thread is the part of the join that must be managed in the tatting process to not be visually distracting. This is especially true if you are joining two different colored elements.

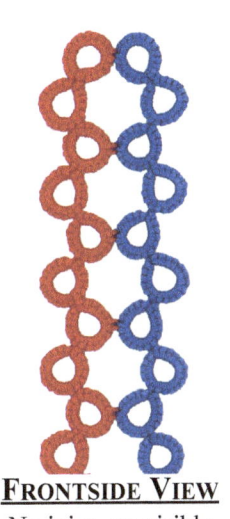
FRONTSIDE VIEW
No joins are visible

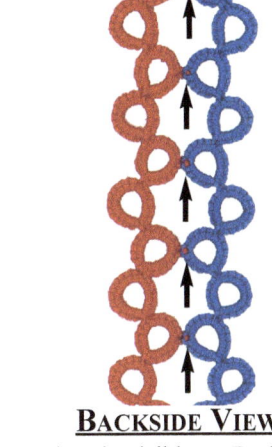
BACKSIDE VIEW
Rnd 1, red joining picot is visible on Rnd 2, blue work *(arrows)*

If you are joining different-colored elements together & if you choose to NOT to use Frontside/Backside Tatting Technique in your work, , then you will need to choose one side of your work to be the 'backside'.

Choose the appropriate Join (Up or Down) to use to ensure that all the horizontal spaces of the joining picot are at one side of the piece.

For a more comprehensive review of Frontside/Backside Tatting see **Fun with Split Ring Tatting** *in which four pages are devoted this topic.*

Tatting Join Techniques (2)

1. The Traditional Join (also known as an **Up Join**)---*the thread loop is brought **UP** through the picot.*
2. A newer way to join is known as a **Down Join**--*the thread loop is brought **DOWN** through the picot.*

Both techniques join two elements together. How and when they are used can produce different visual effects due to where the extra horizontal thread ends up--either on the front or backside of the elements.

Up Join

Lay the picot on top of the thread of the element you are joining together.

The working thread is brought **UP** and through the picot, the shuttle passed through the loop of thread formed, and the join nestled down into position. *ILLUS A*

This join method is sometimes called a 'Frontside Join' because the horizontal space of thread is toward the 'backside' of the piece/element and does not distract from the 'frontside' of the work. In other words, the 'frontside' is visually preserved.

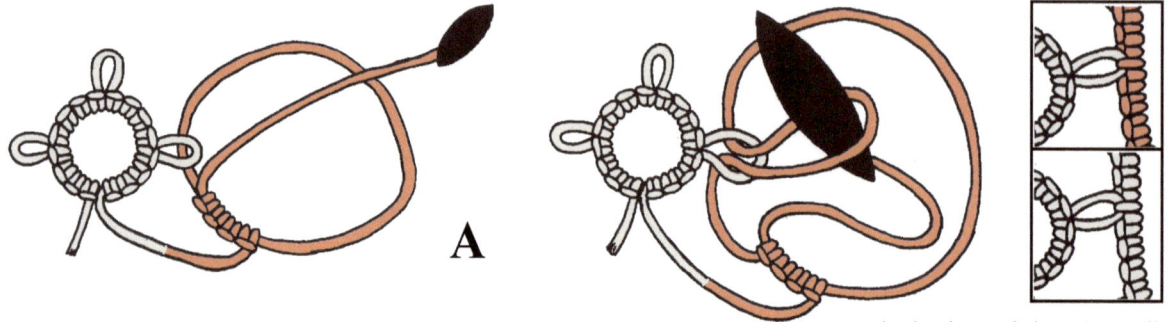

The horizontal thread supplied by the picot is on the ***backside*** of the work.

Down Join

Lay the picot below the thread of the element you are joining together.

The thread is brought **DOWN** and through the picot, the shuttle passed through the loop of thread formed, and the join nestled down into position. *ILLUS B*

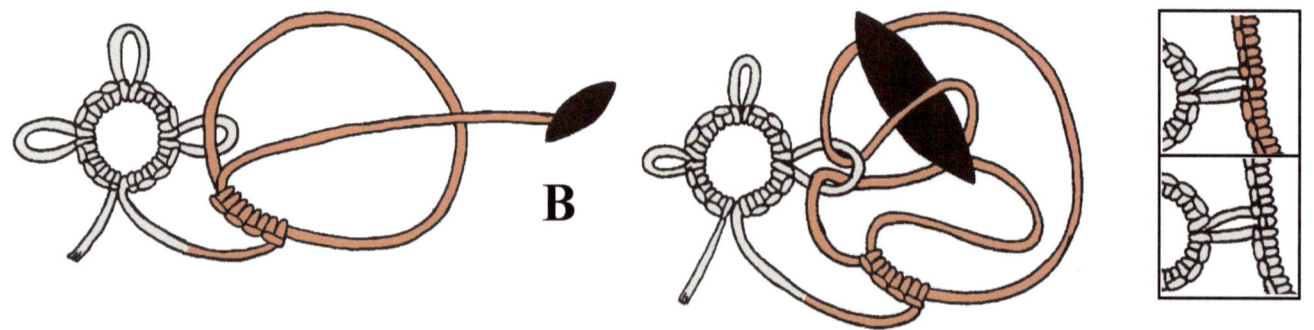

The horizontal thread supplied by the picot is on the ***frontside*** of the work.

Variables that Dictate Which tatting Join Technique *(Up or Down)* to Use

--Current tatting theory contends that the horizontal space of thread on the frontside, when finished with an Over Stitch, most closely matches the appearance of a regular double stitch.

--Frontside versus backside tatting:
> To match in appearance, frontside elements are joined with an Up Join while backside elements are joined with a Down Join. The Up Join is opposite of a Down Join. Because the element is reversed to being worked as a backside element, the joining technique is also reversed.

--Joining different colored elements.
> The horizontal space of thread can be a distraction when joining an element of one color to a picot of another color. Thus when joining two different-colored elements, a different approach is used compared to one-color tatting.

Traditional Approach to Joining Technique

When Tatting An Element As	&	Elements Being Joined Together Are	Use	Follow the Join with an
Frontside		One Color	Down Join	Over Half Stitch
Backside		One Color	Up Join	Under Half Stitch
Frontside		Two Colors	Up Join	Over Half Stitch
Backside		Two Colors	Down Join	Under Half Stitch

Modified Approach to Joining Technique

This author has a different approach to joins. She contends that the horizontal space of thread is hard to smooth down. Thus, she uses a joining technique to always place the horizontal bar of picot thread to the backside of the work.

When Tatting An Element As	&	Elements Being Joined Together Are	Use	Follow the Join with an
Frontside		One Color or Two Colors	Up Join	Over Half Stitch
Backside		One Color or Two Colors	Down Join	Under Half Stitch

CHEVRON　　　HERRINGBONE

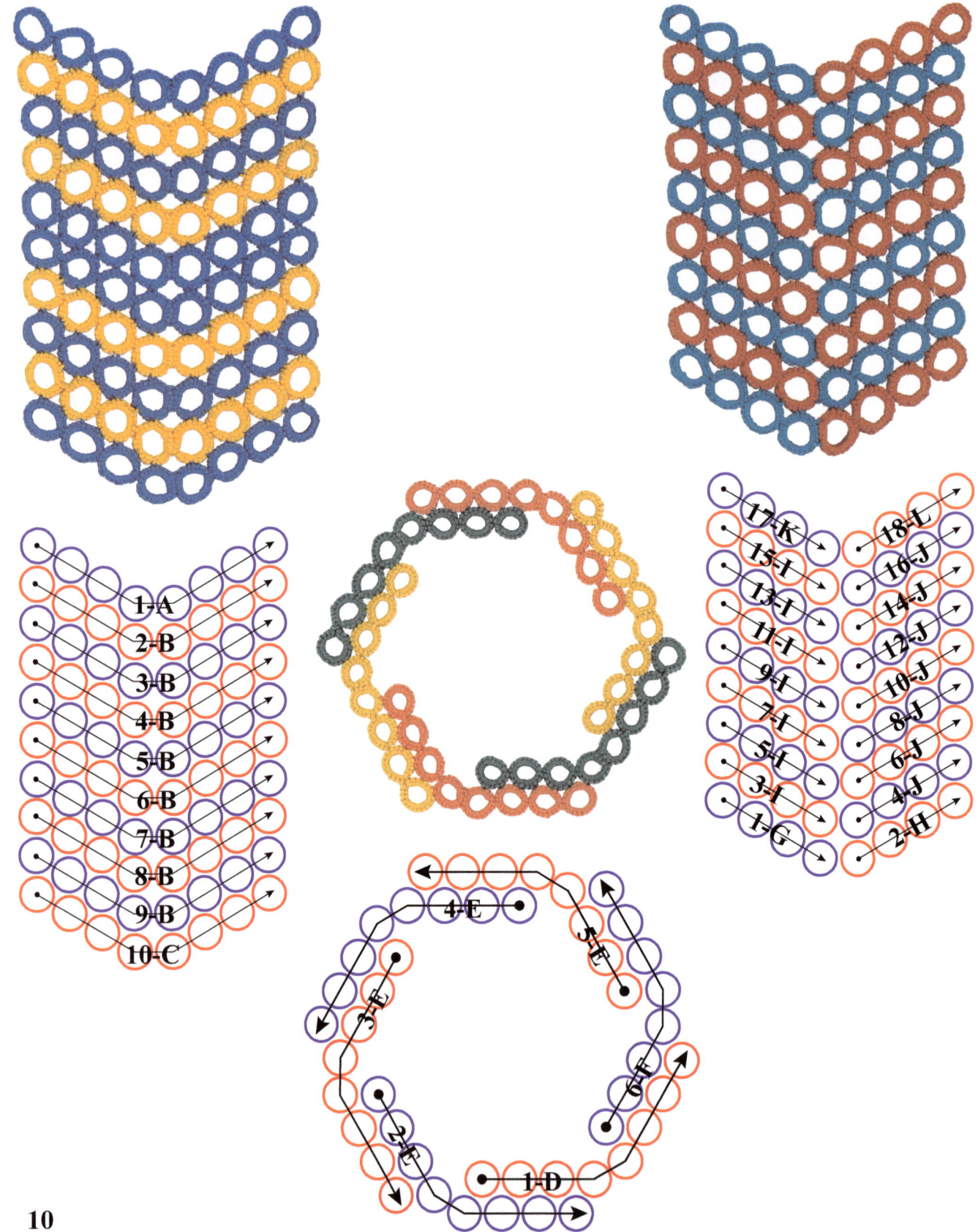

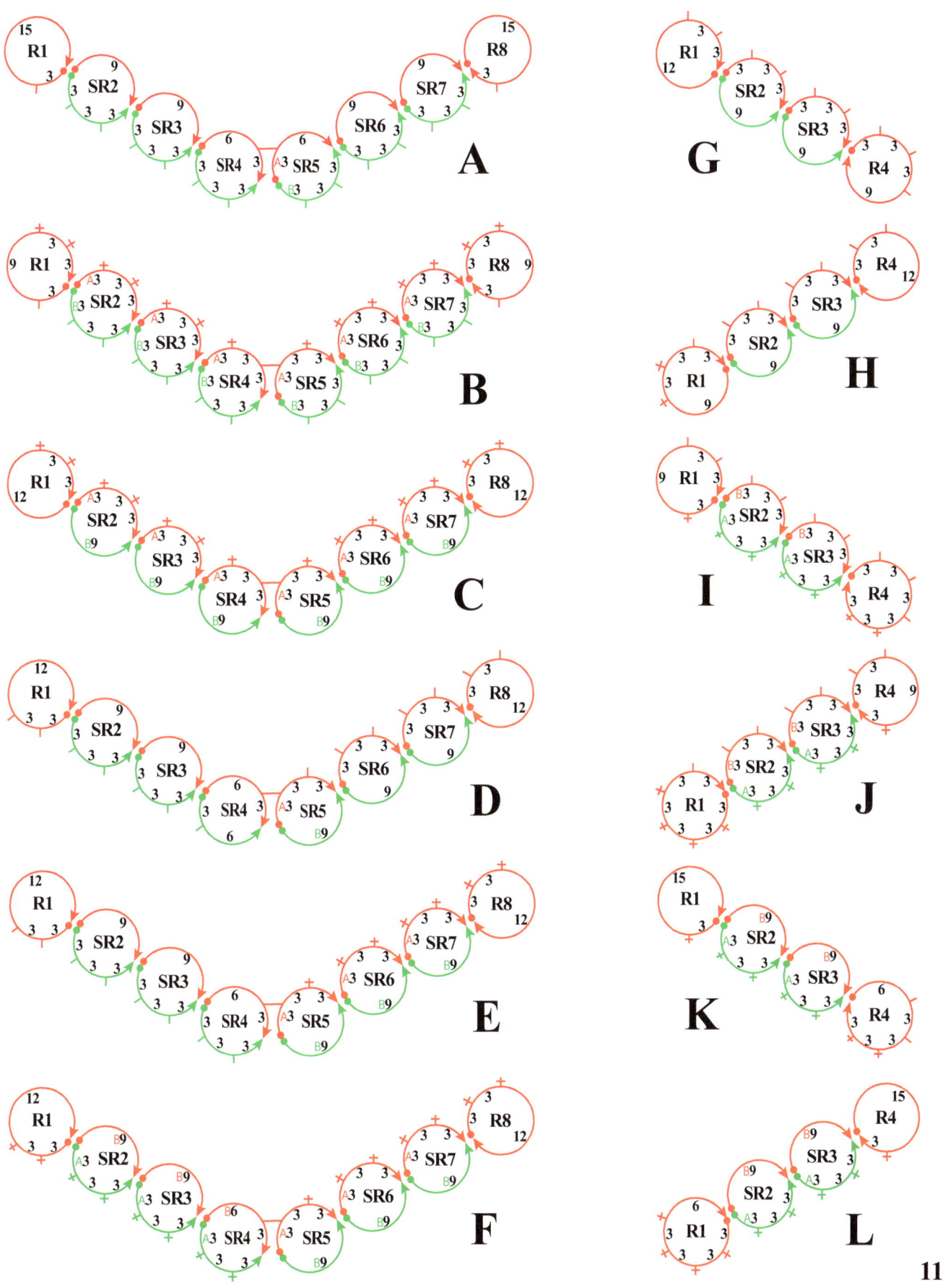

CHEVRON

HEART

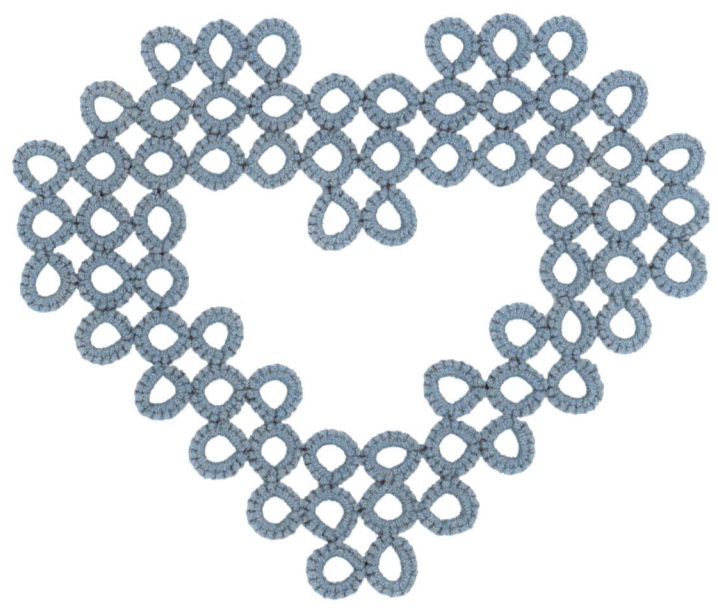

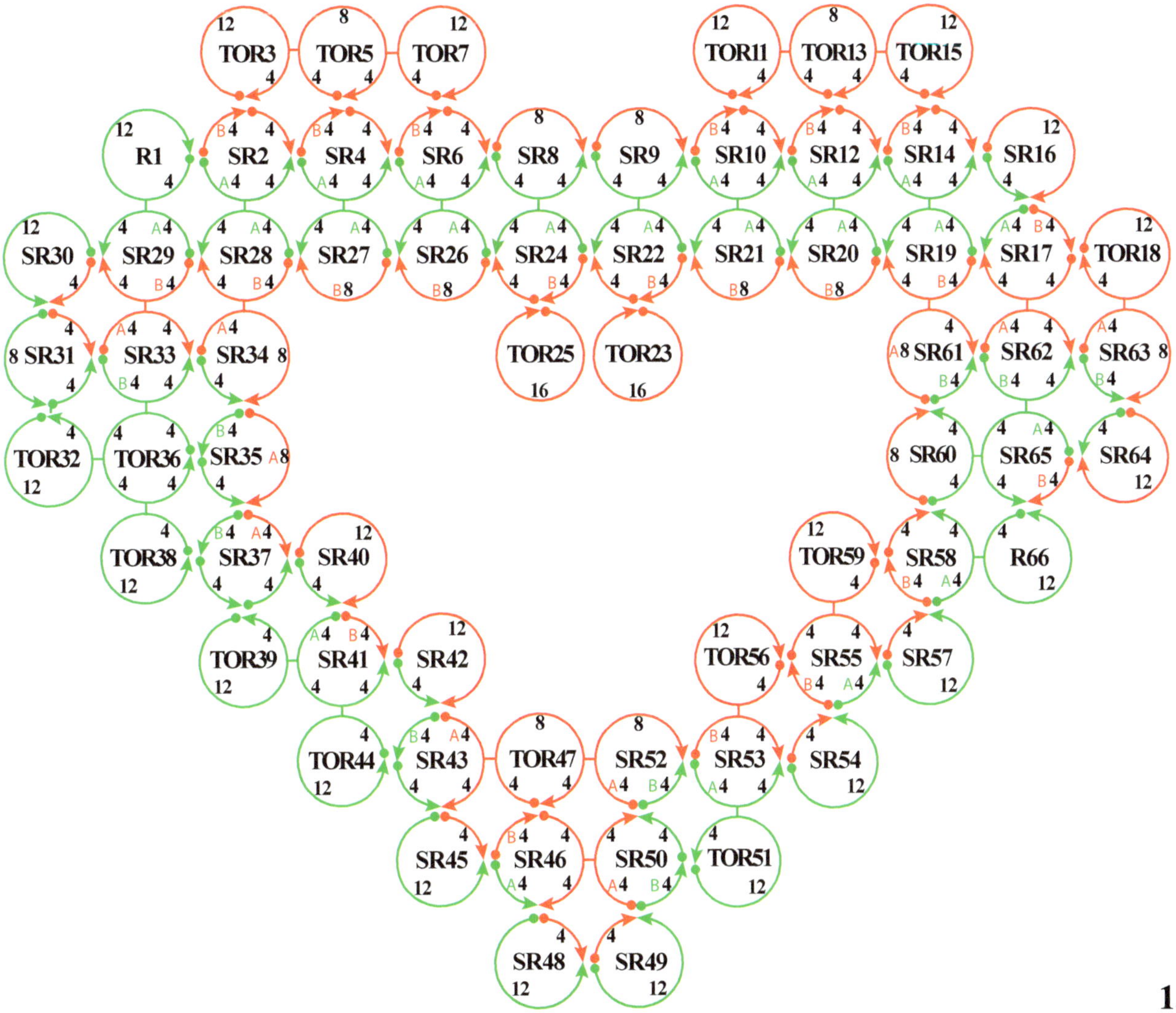
TOR3
TOR5
TOR7
TOR11
TOR13
TOR15
R1
SR2
SR4
SR6
SR8
SR9
SR10
SR12
SR14
SR16
SR30
SR29
SR28
SR27
SR26
SR24
SR22
SR21
SR20
SR19
SR17
TOR18
SR31
SR33
SR34
TOR25
TOR23
SR61
SR62
SR63
TOR32
TOR36
SR35
SR60
SR65
SR64
TOR38
SR37
SR40
TOR59
SR58
R66
TOR39
SR41
SR42
TOR56
SR55
SR57
TOR44
SR43
TOR47
SR52
SR53
SR54
SR45
SR46
SR50
TOR51
SR48
SR49

CELTIC INSPIRED DESIGNS

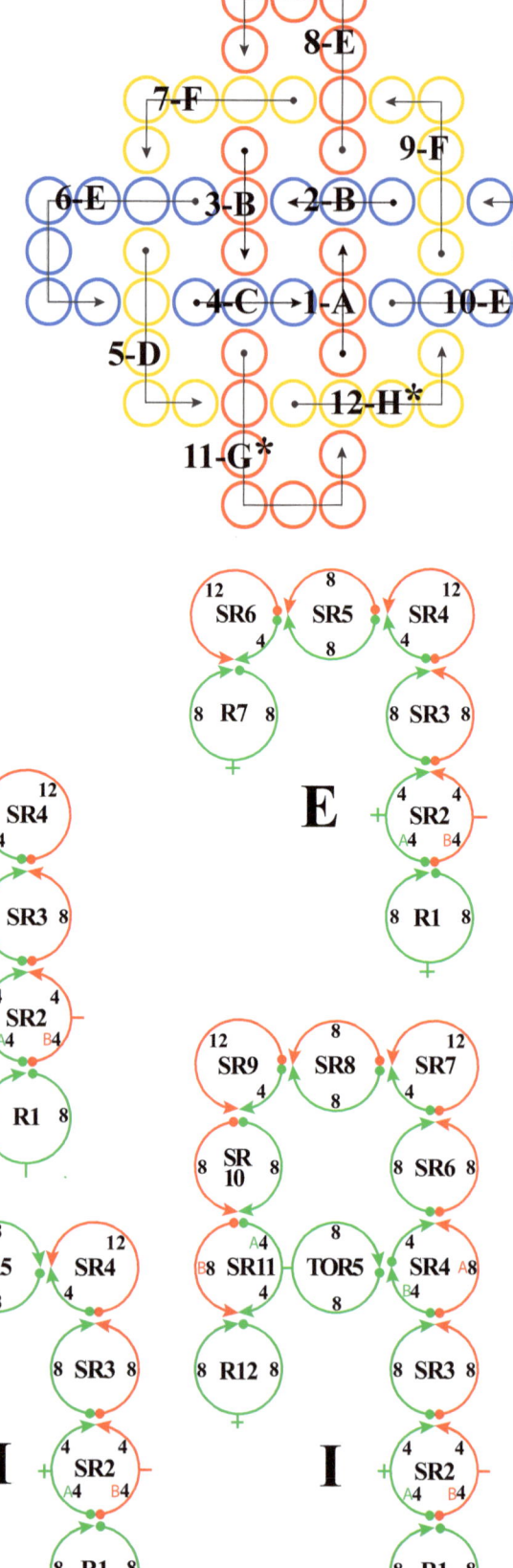

* To avoid use/need of SRJoin Technique:
Work Section 11-G up to SR6.
Then work all of Section 12-H.
Then work Section 11-G, R7.

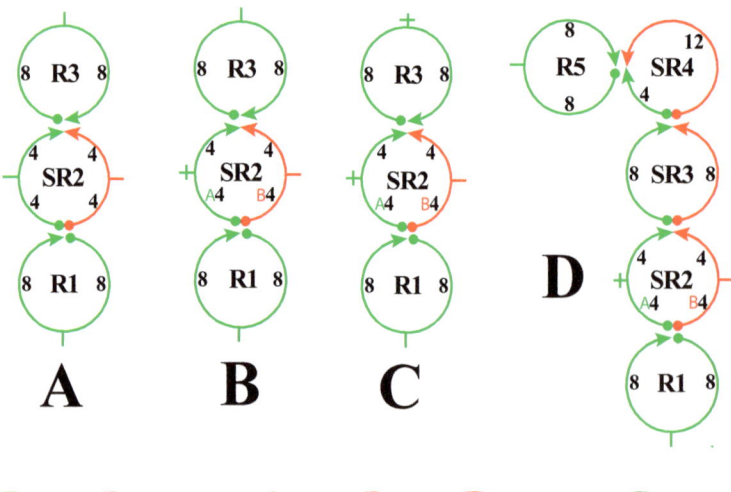

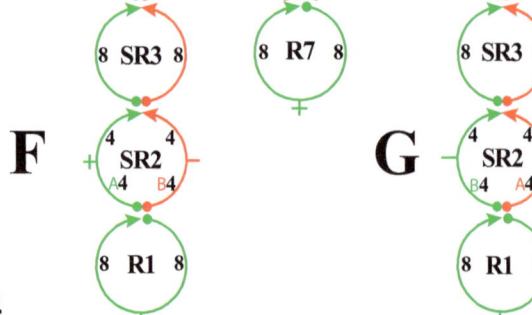

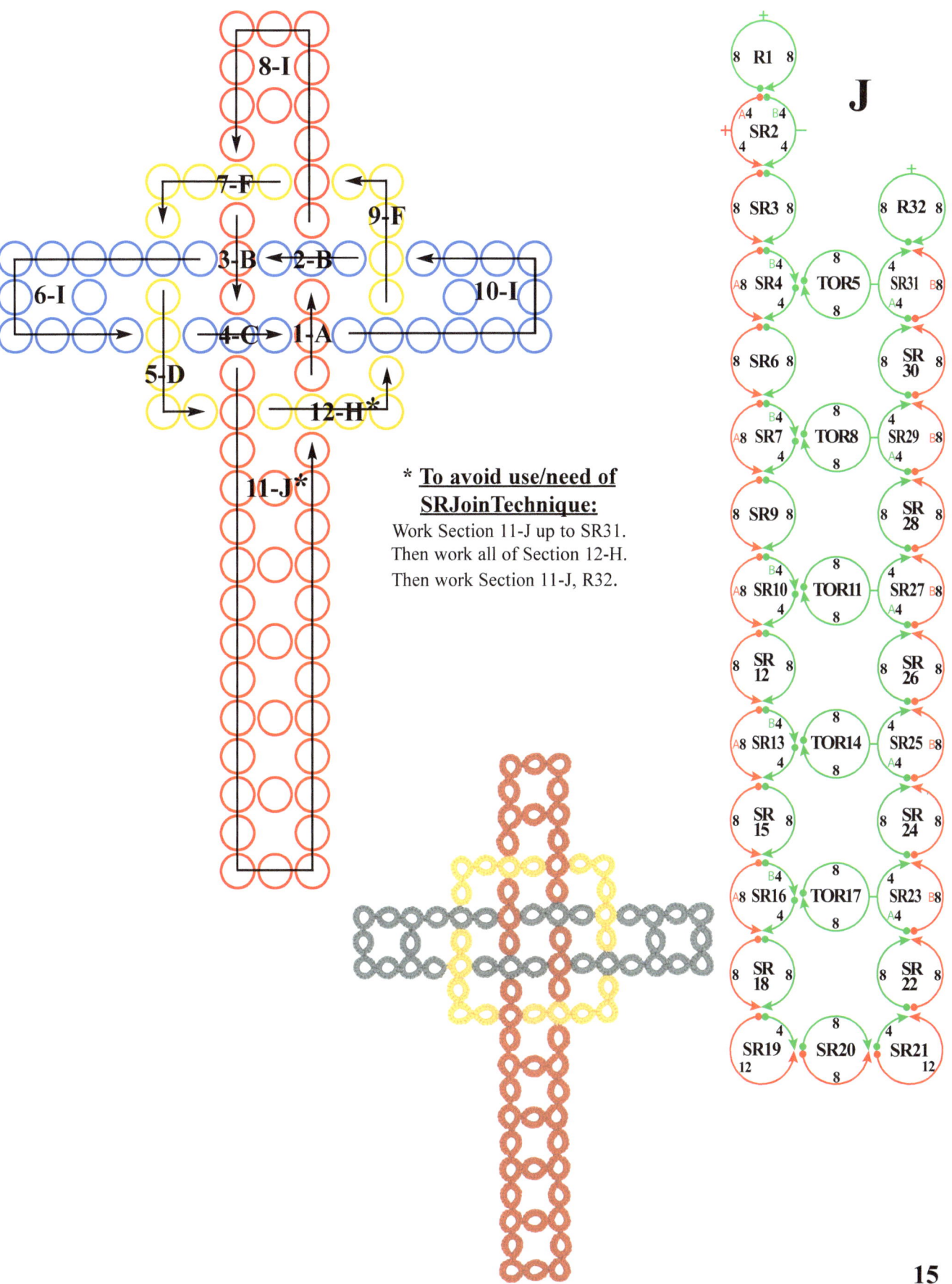

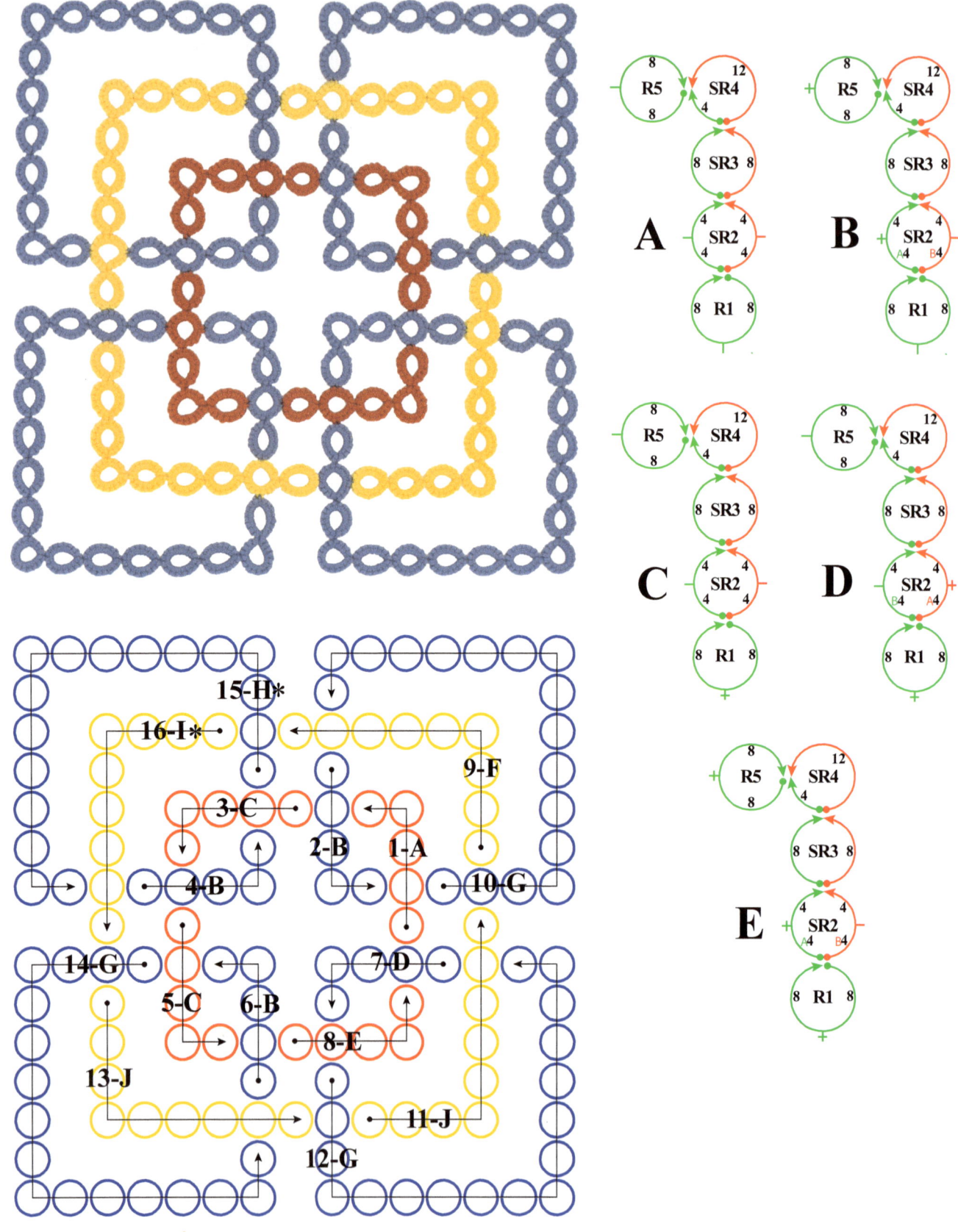

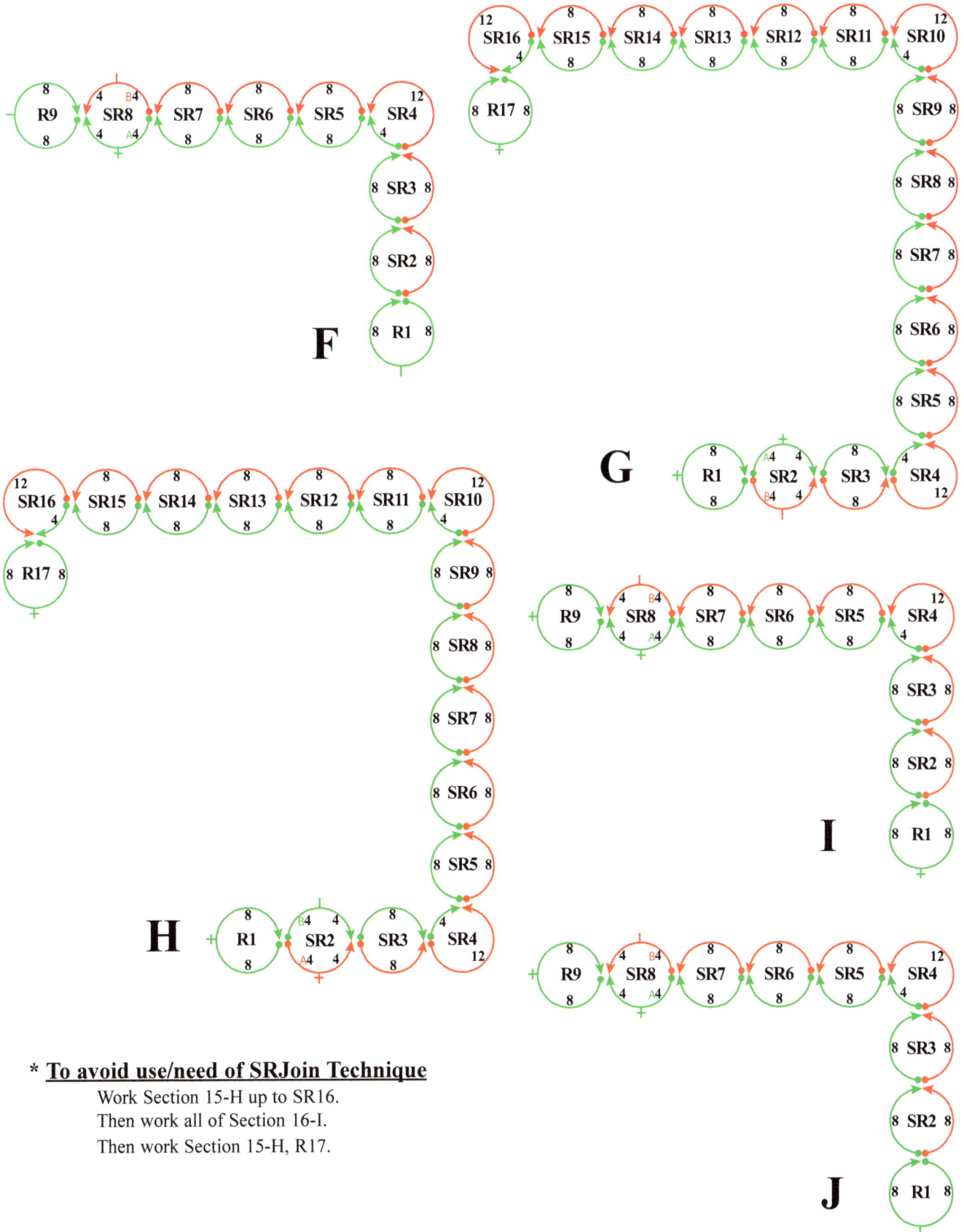

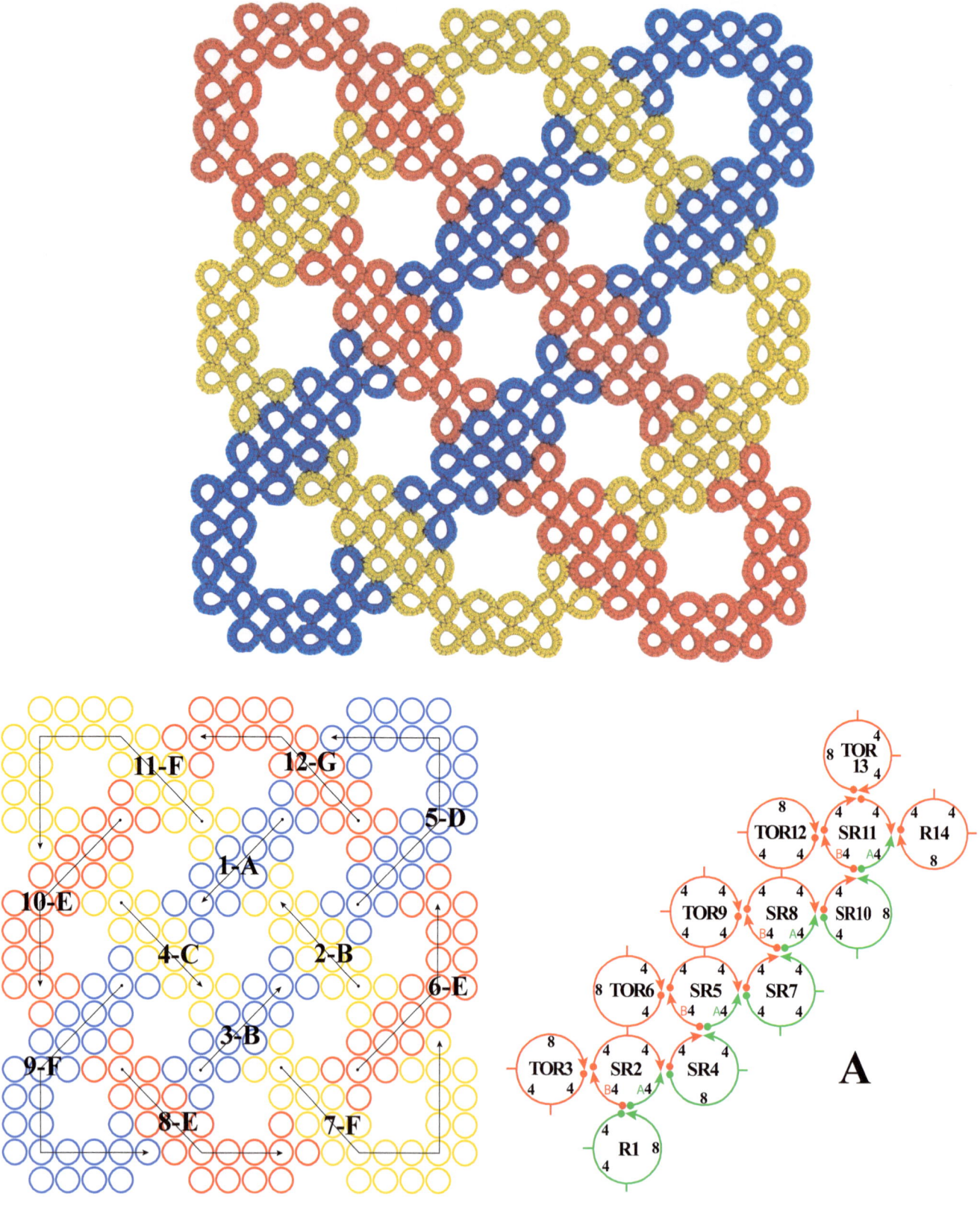

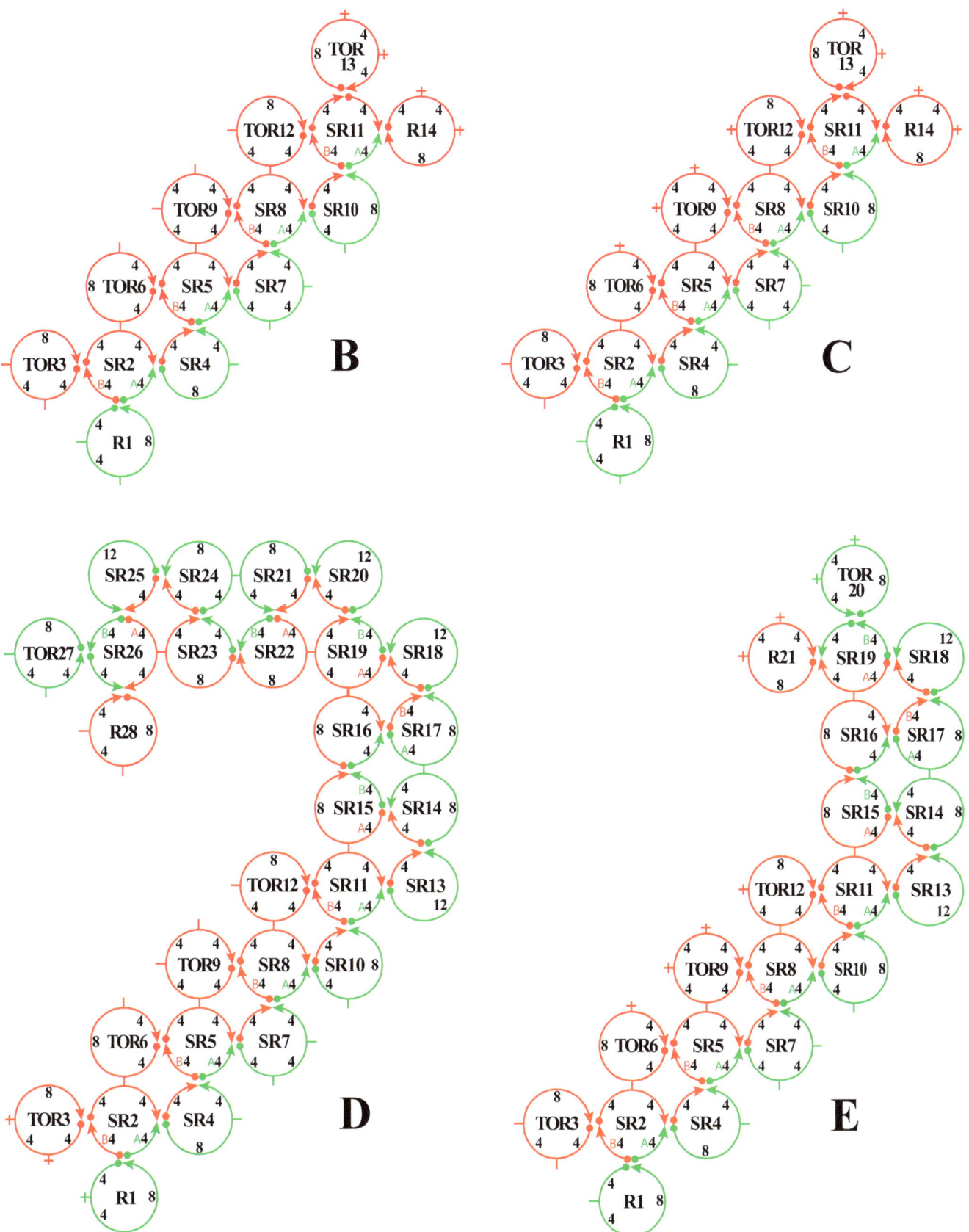

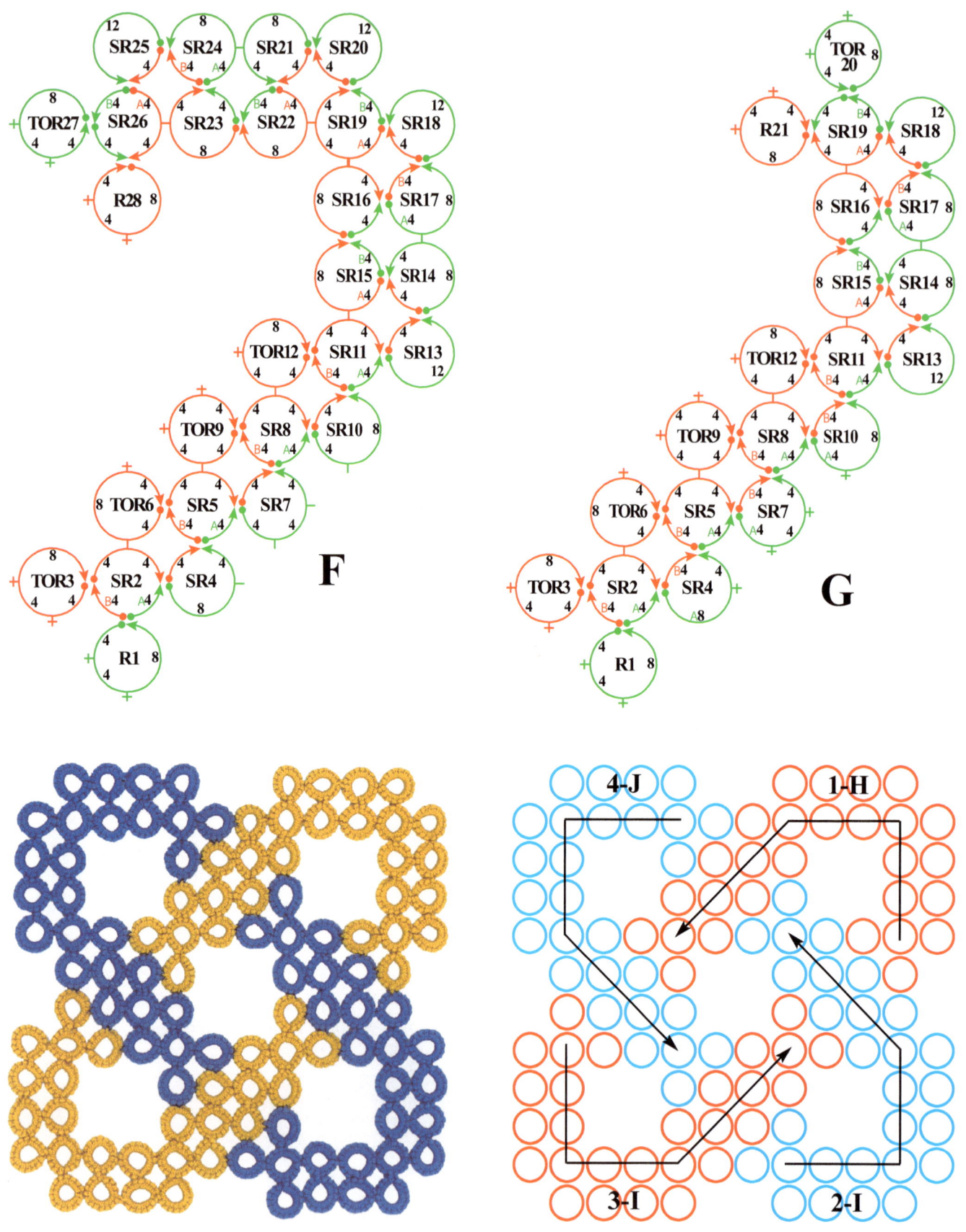

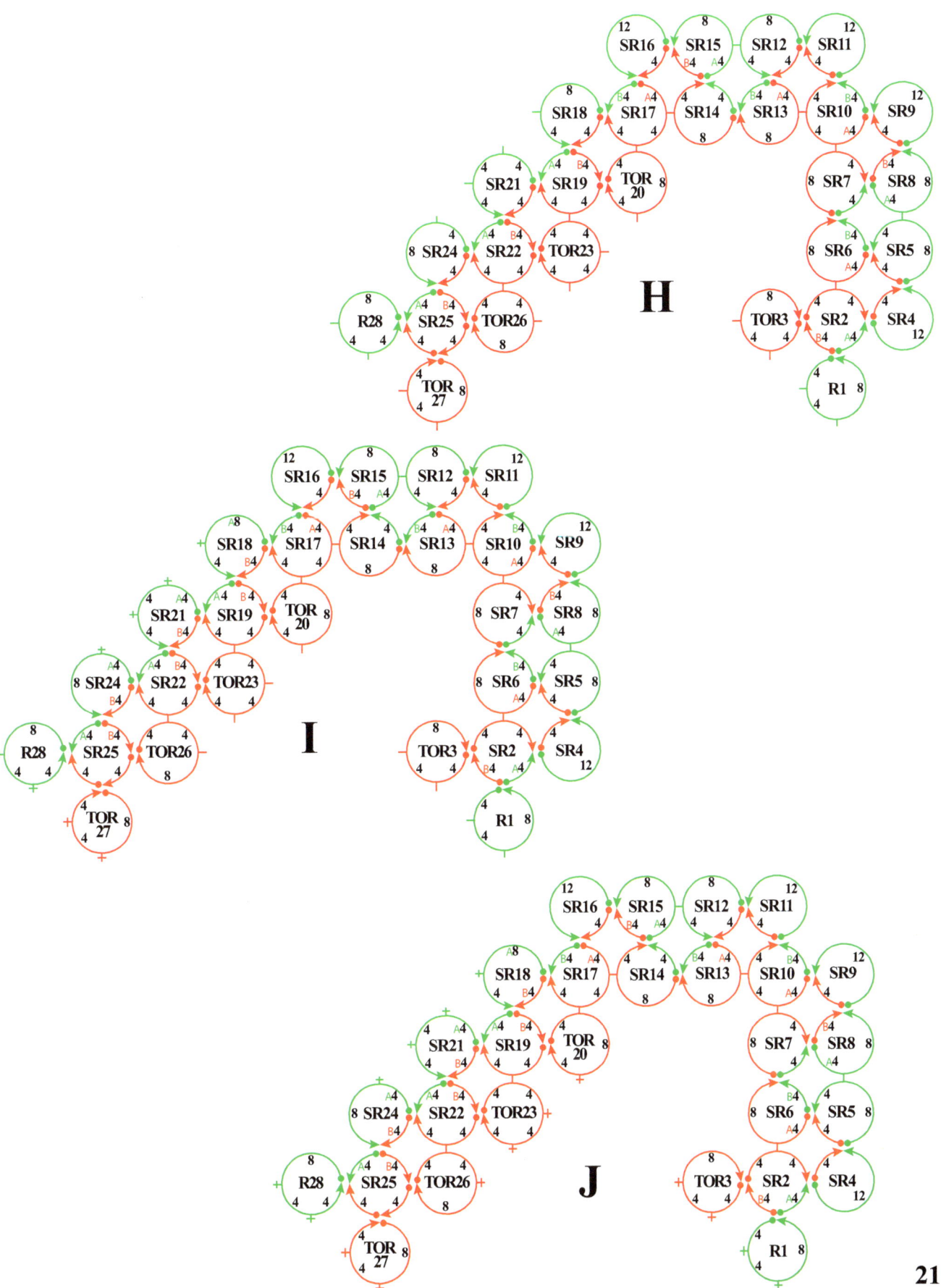

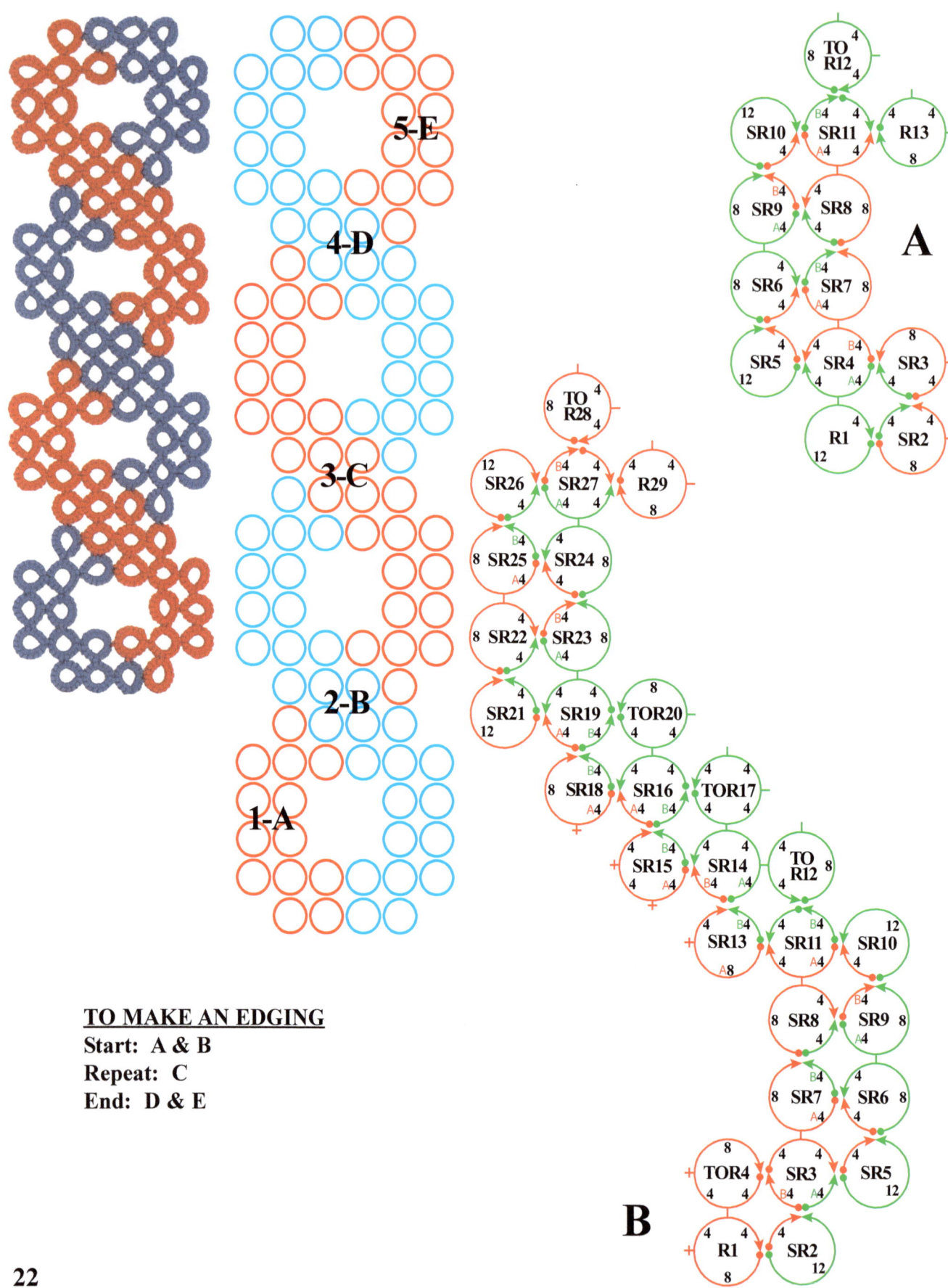

TO MAKE AN EDGING
Start: A & B
Repeat: C
End: D & E

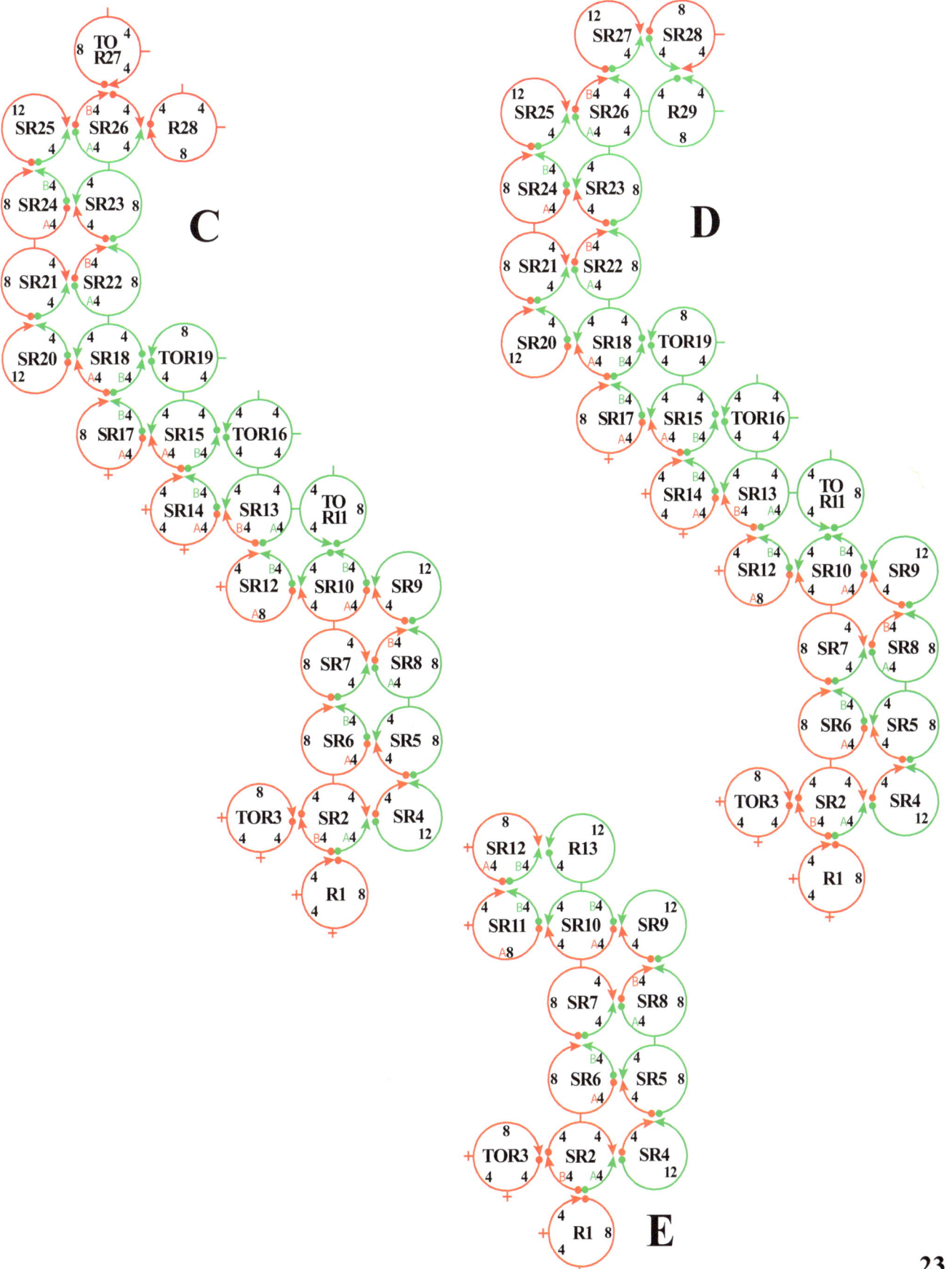

TESSELLATION INSPIRED DESIGNS

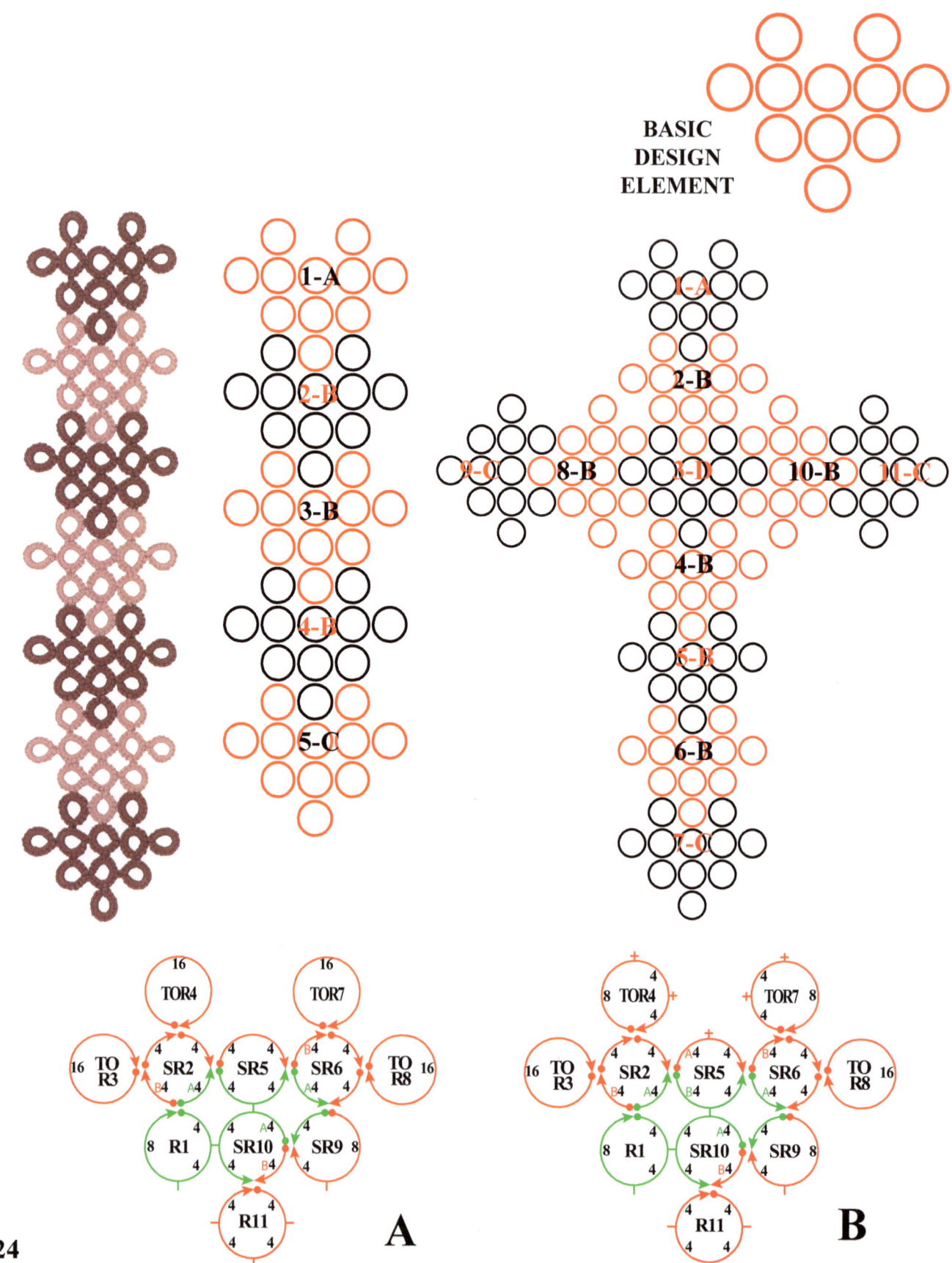

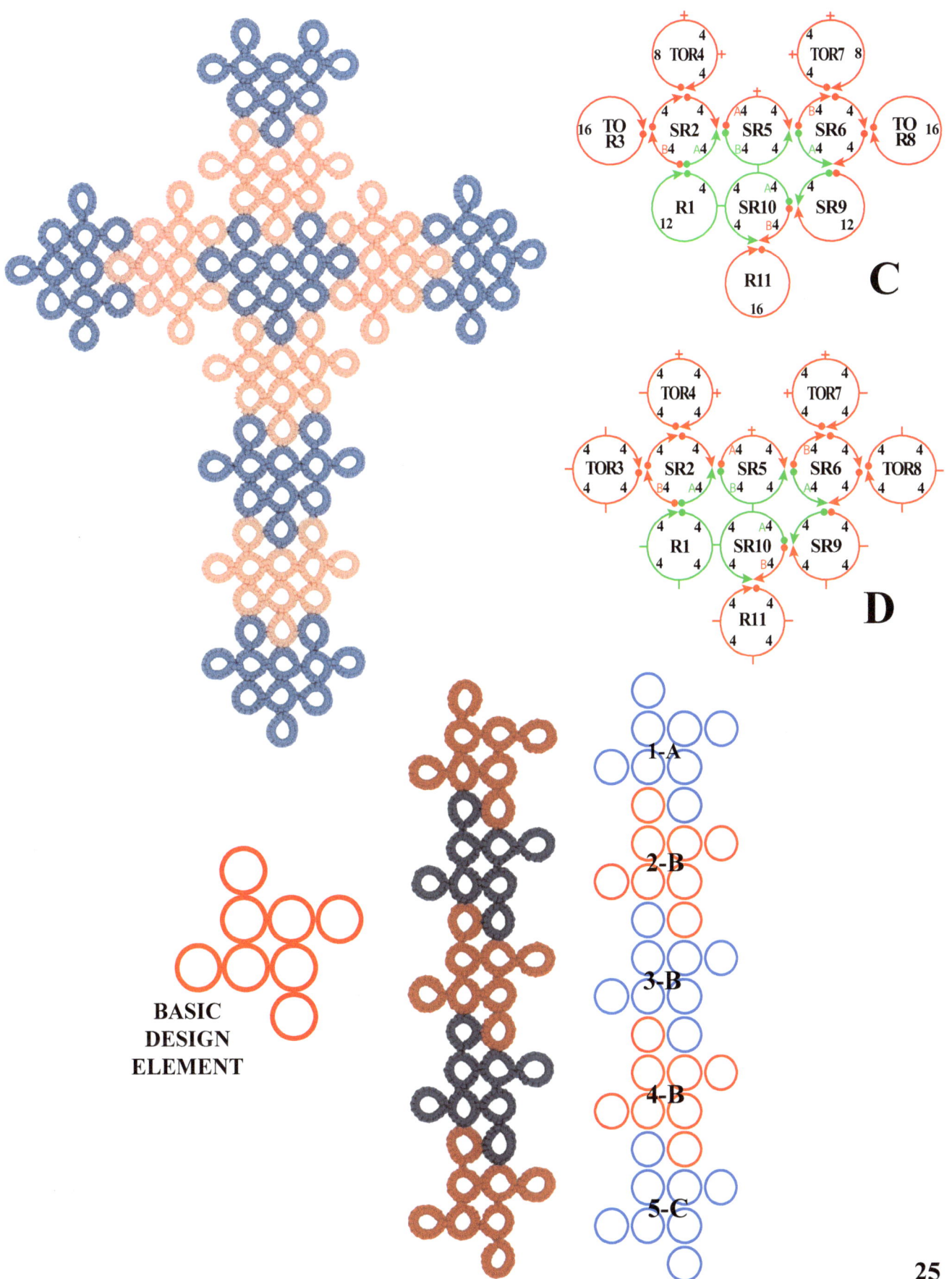

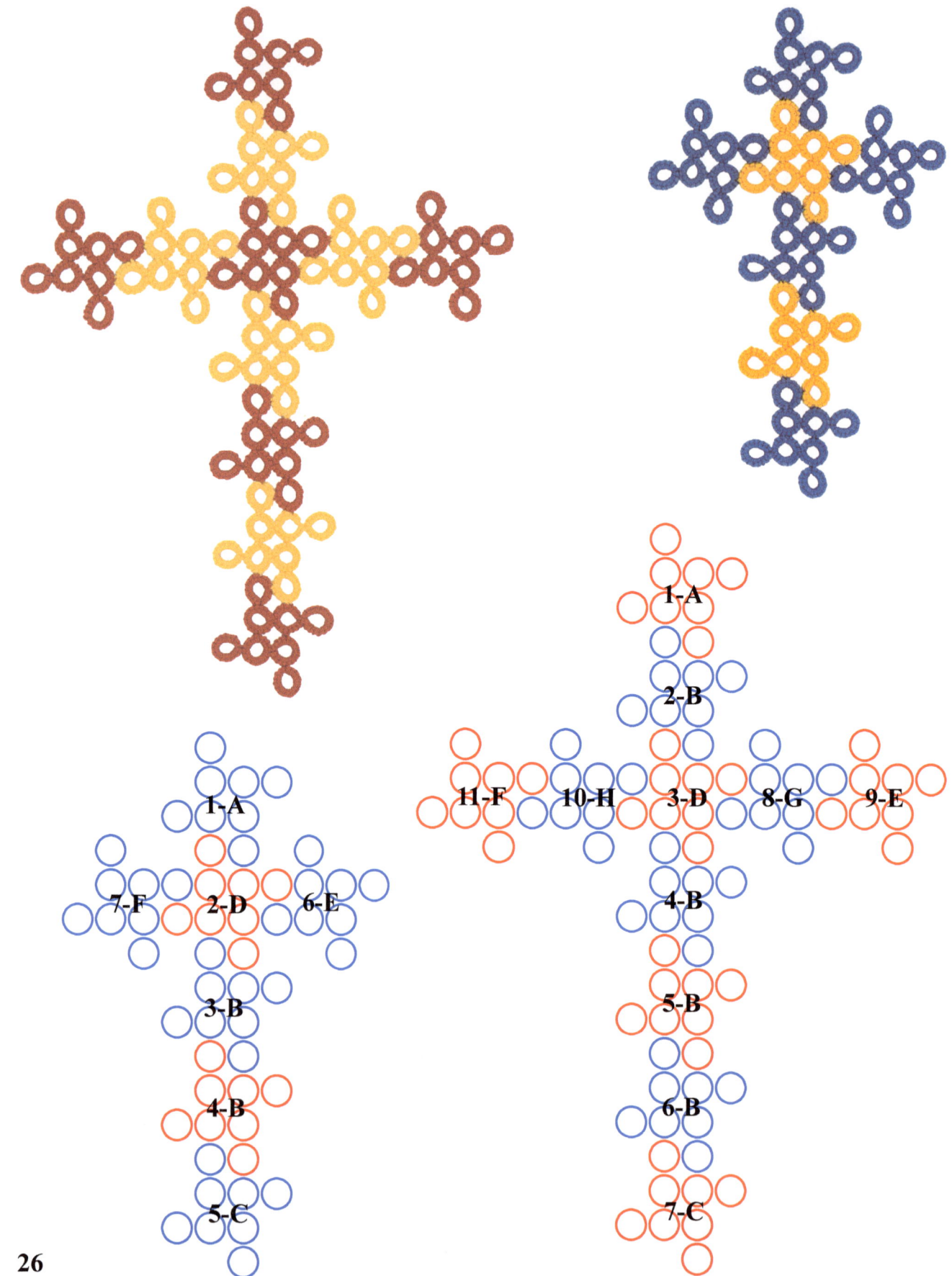

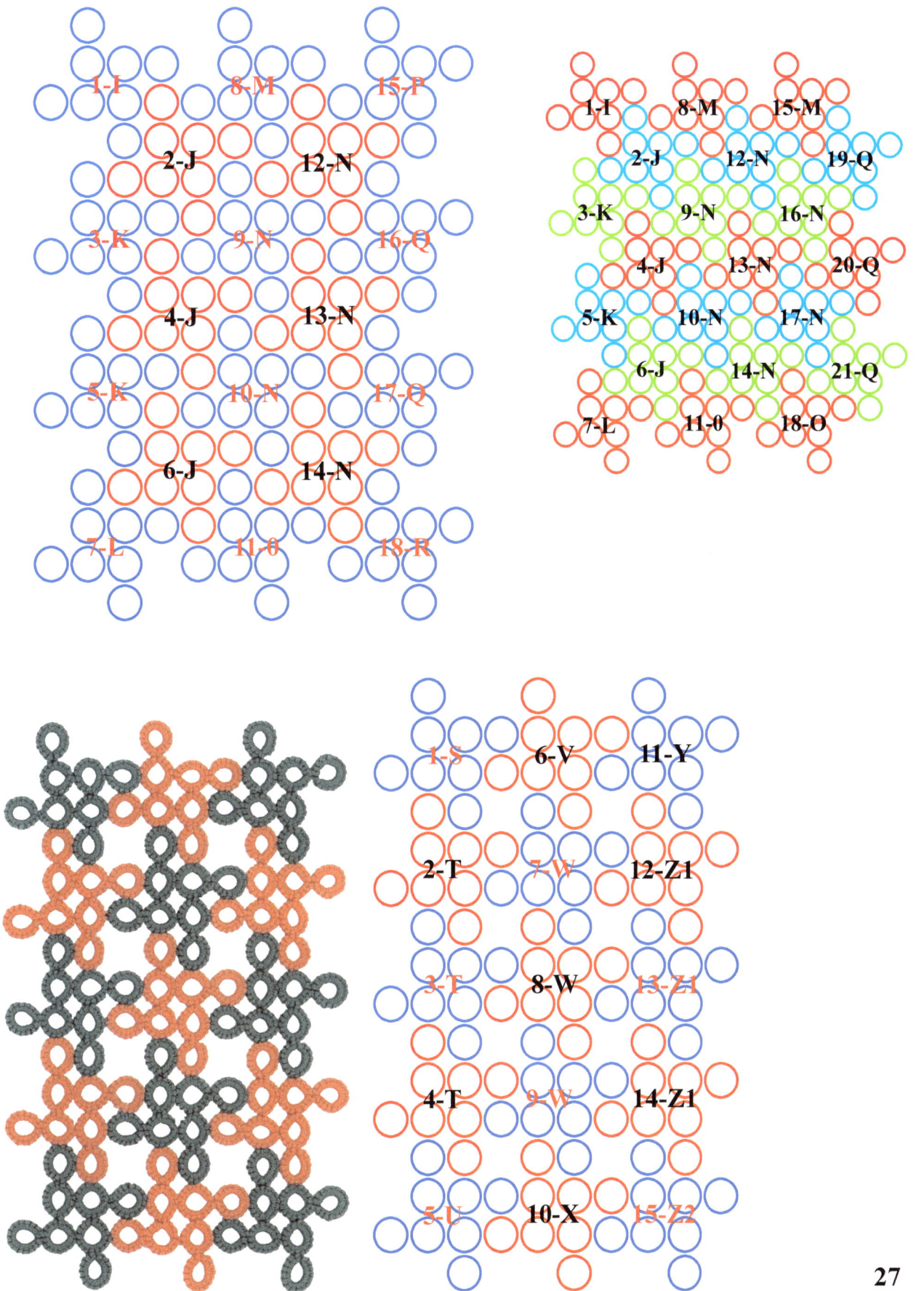

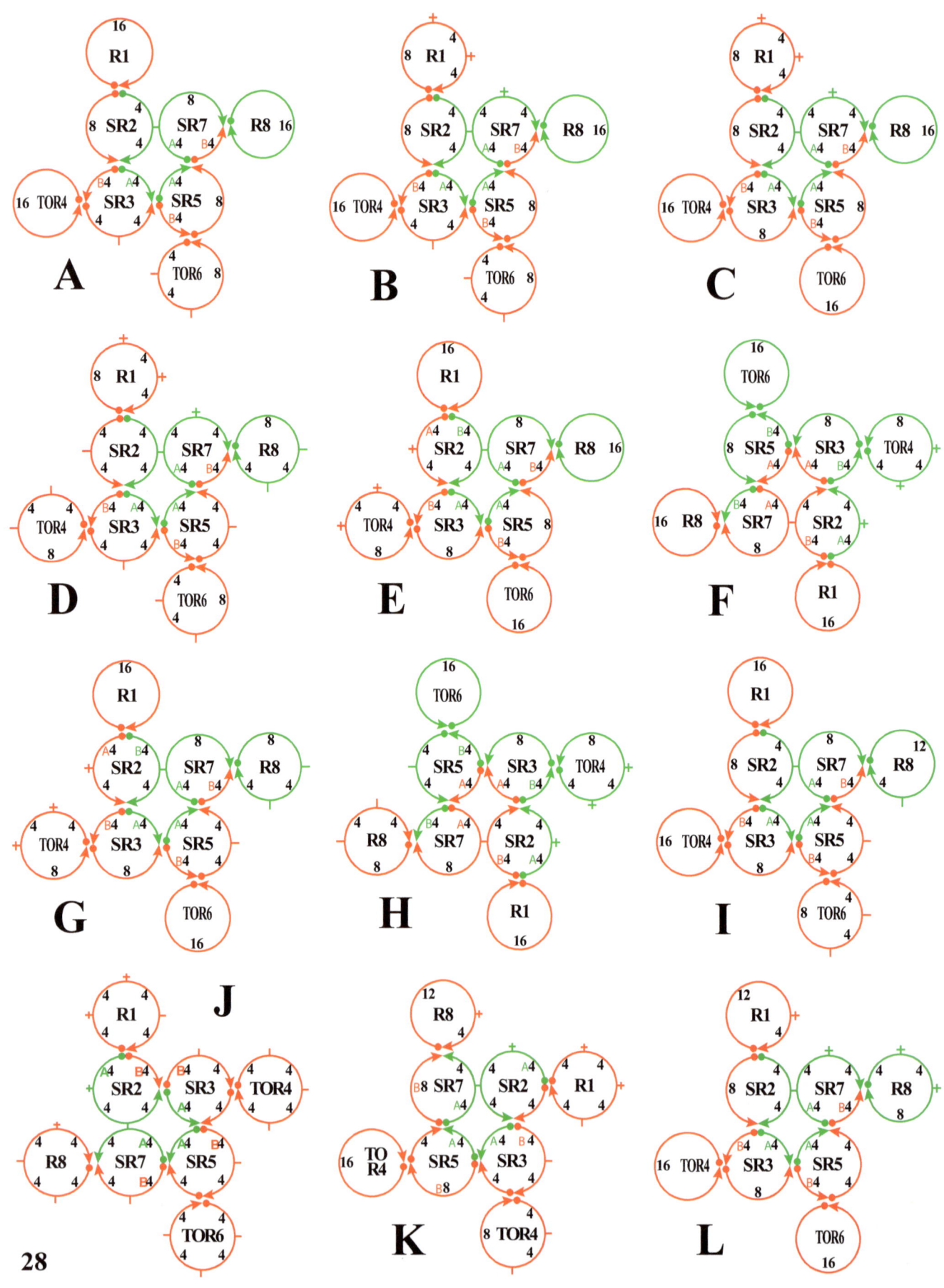

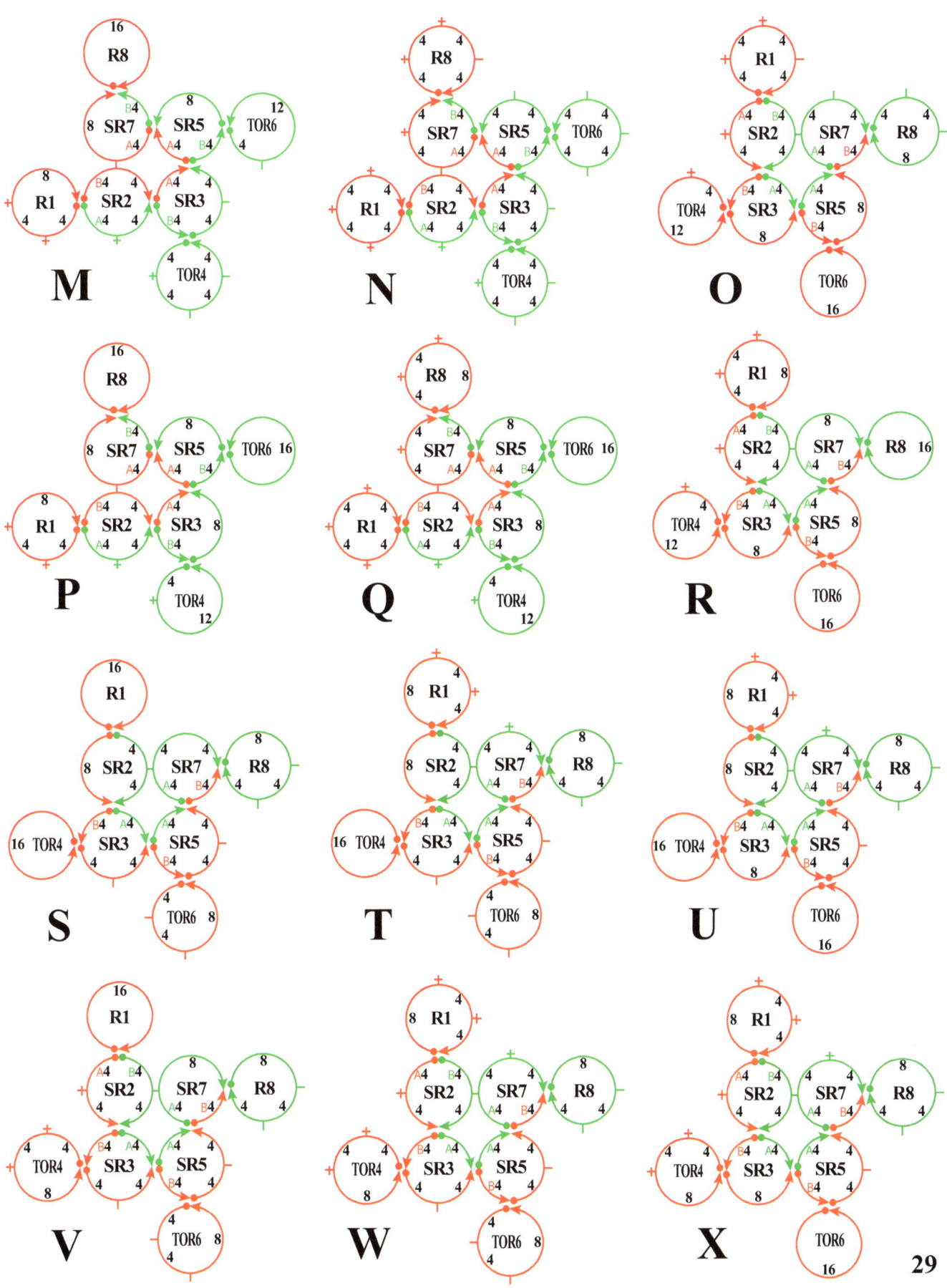

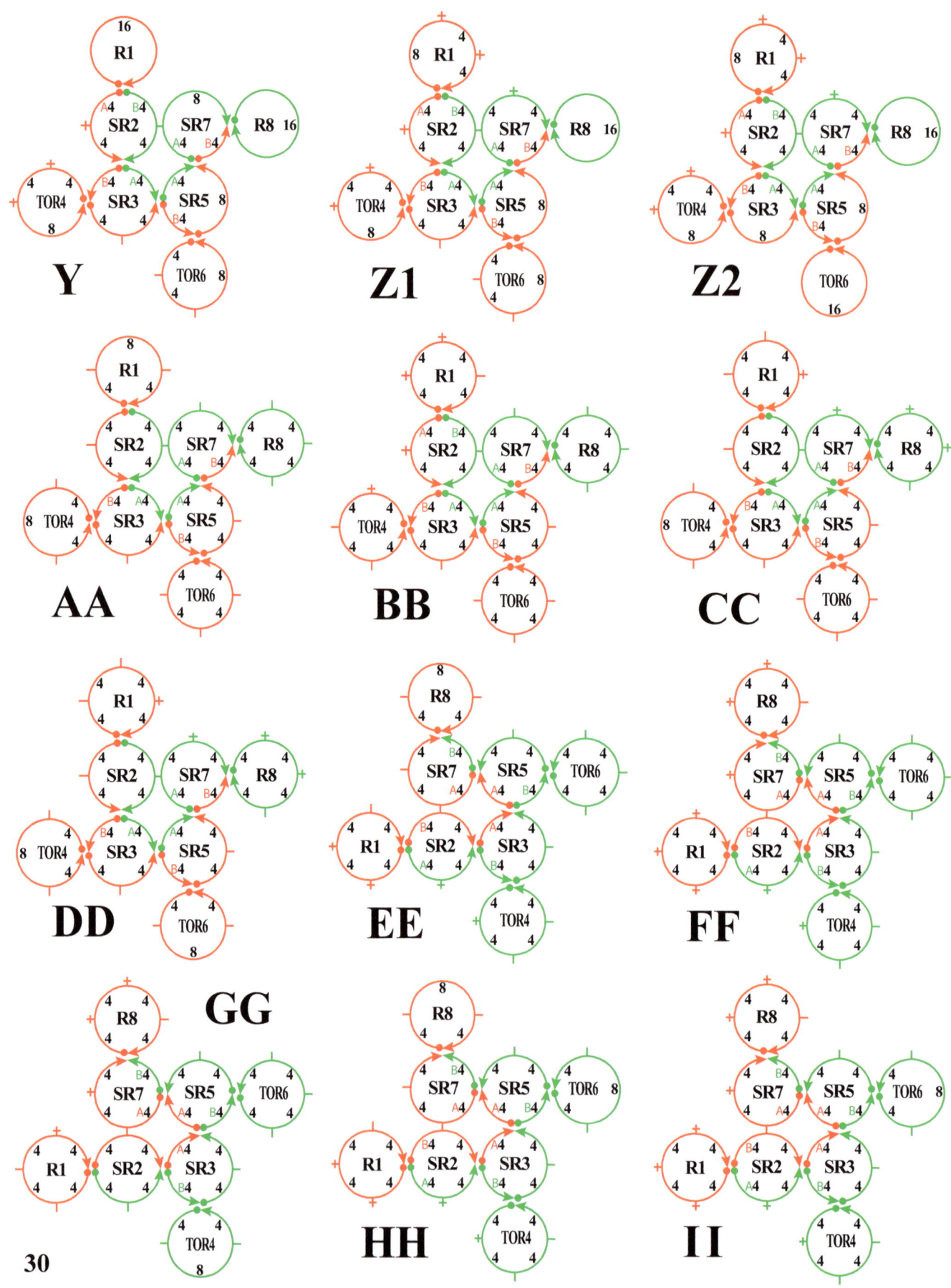

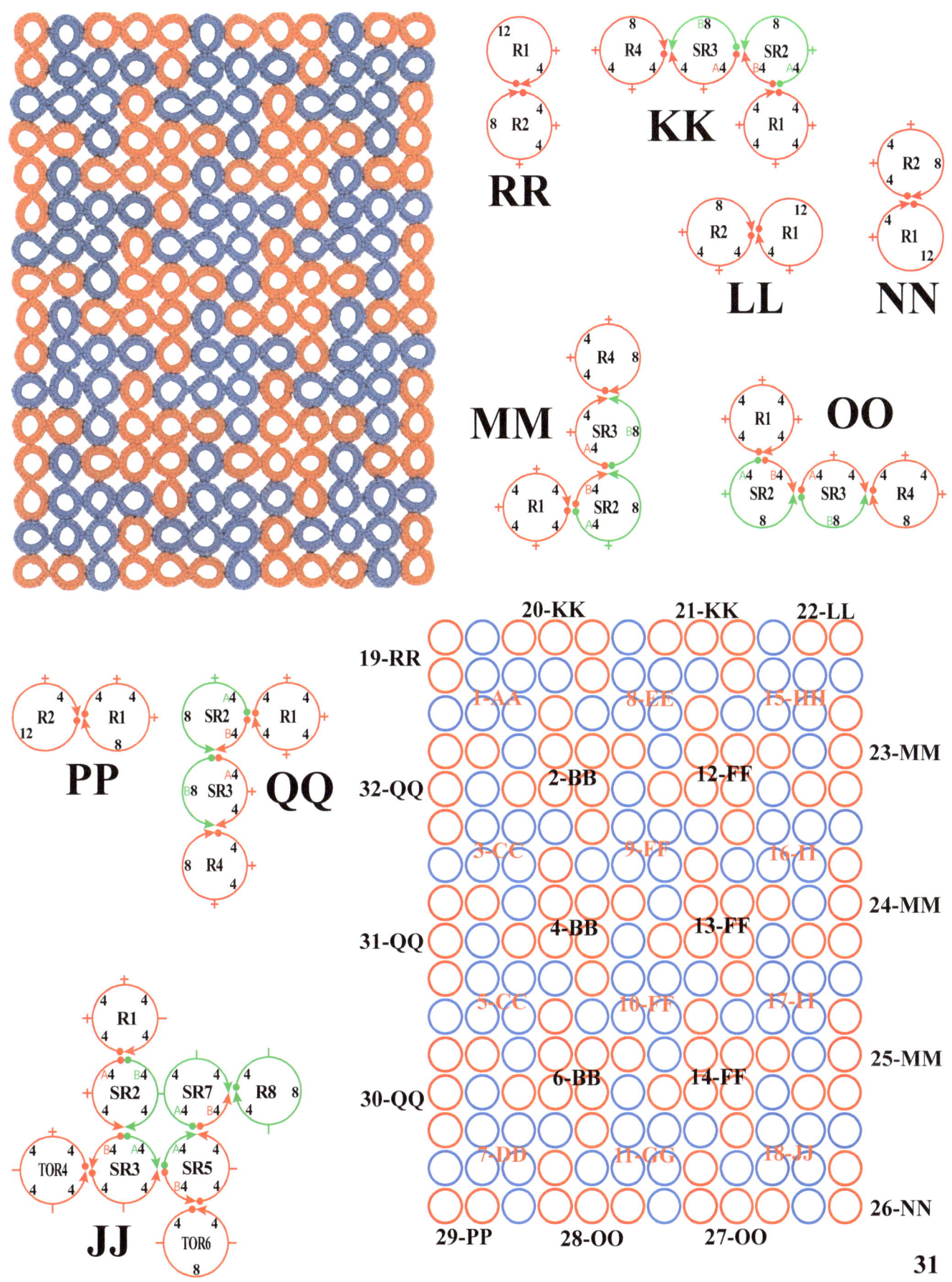

BASIC DESIGN ELEMENTS

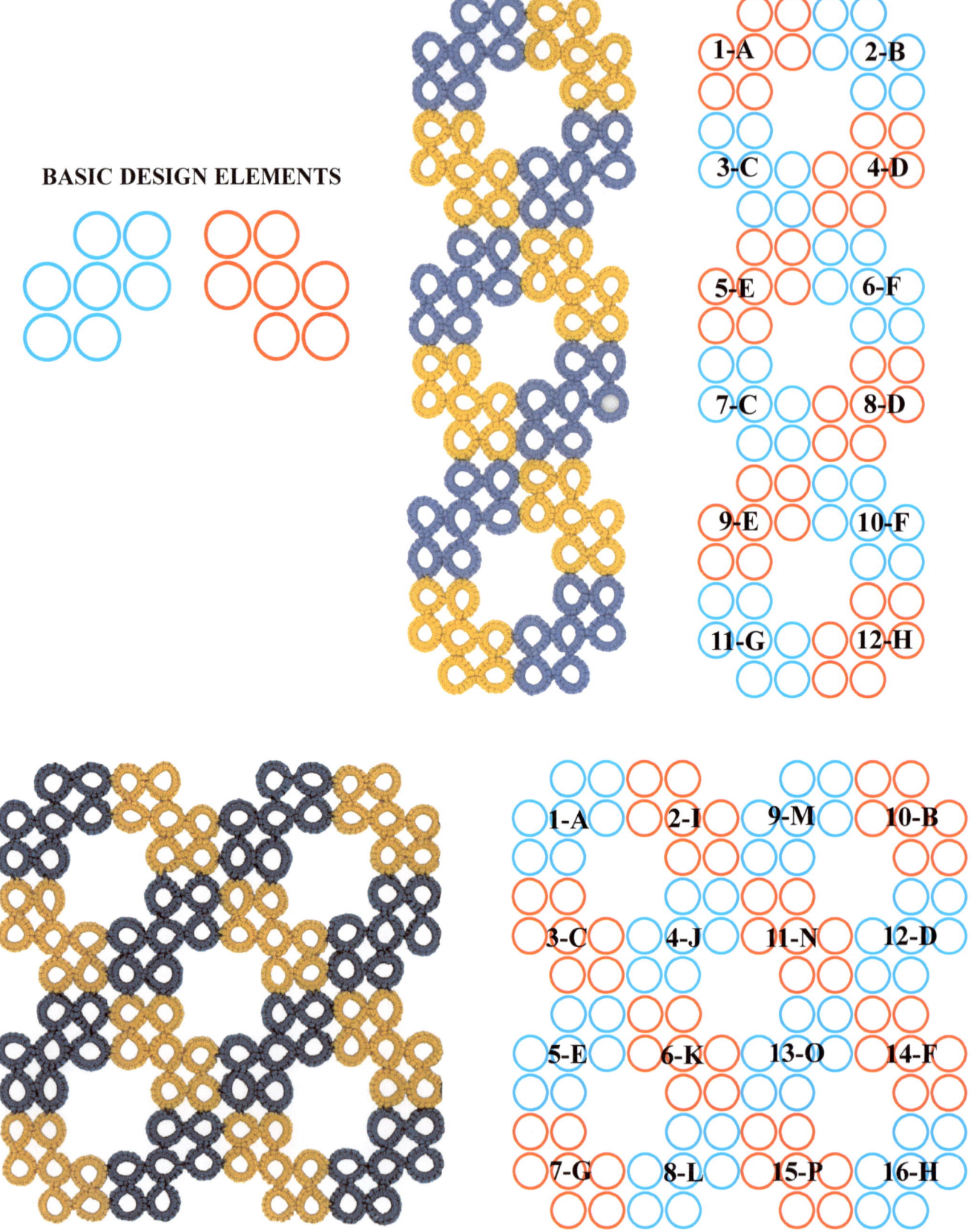

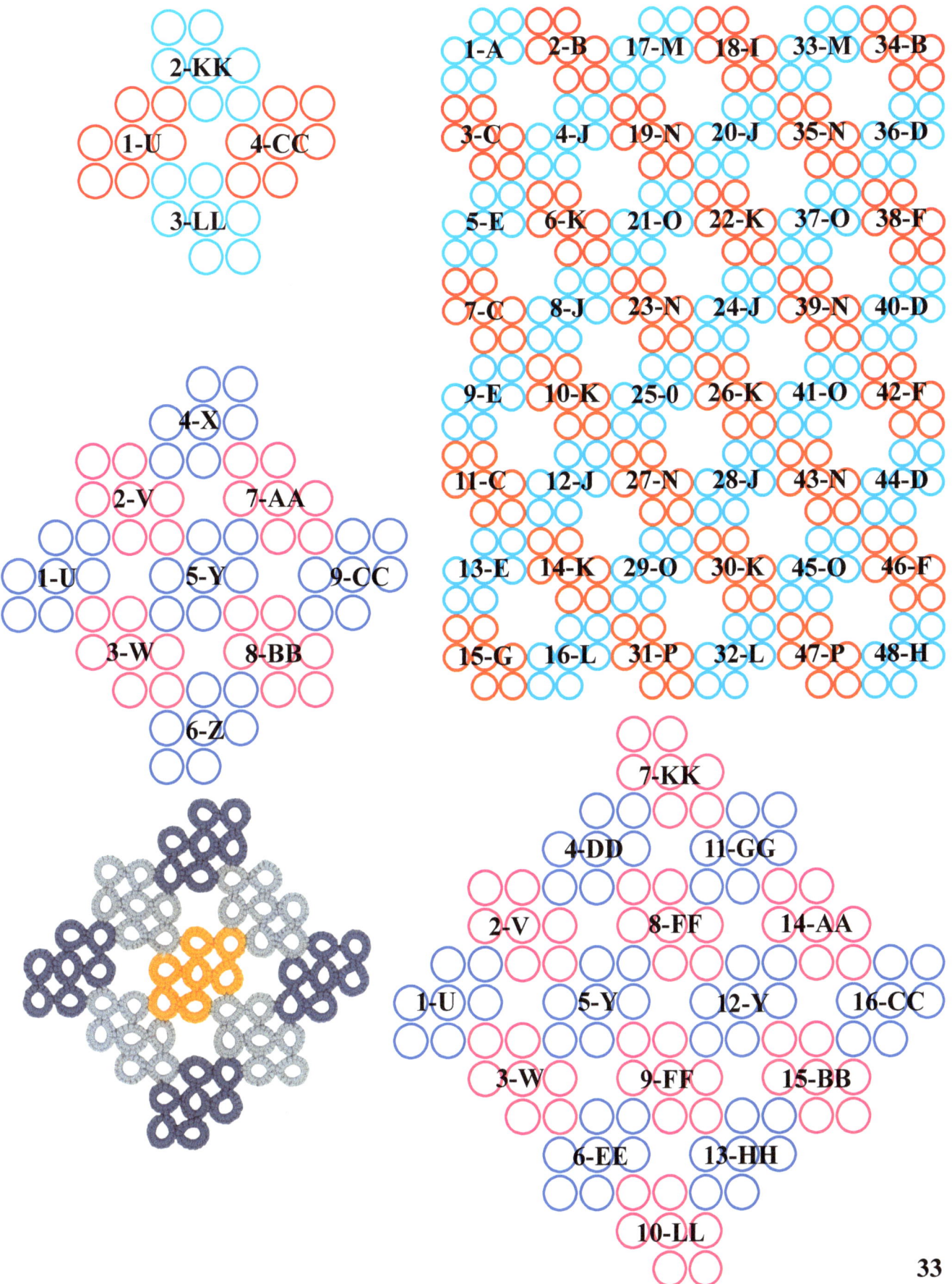

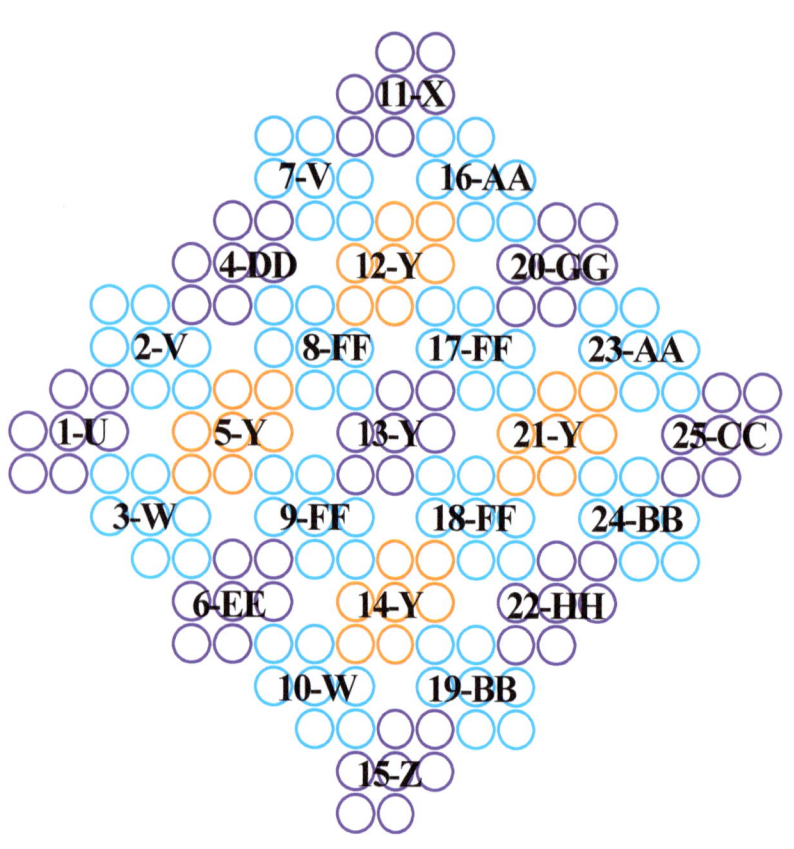

COLOR VARIATION

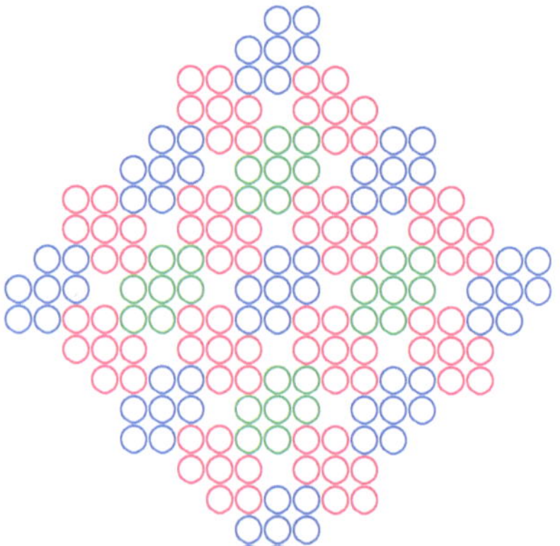

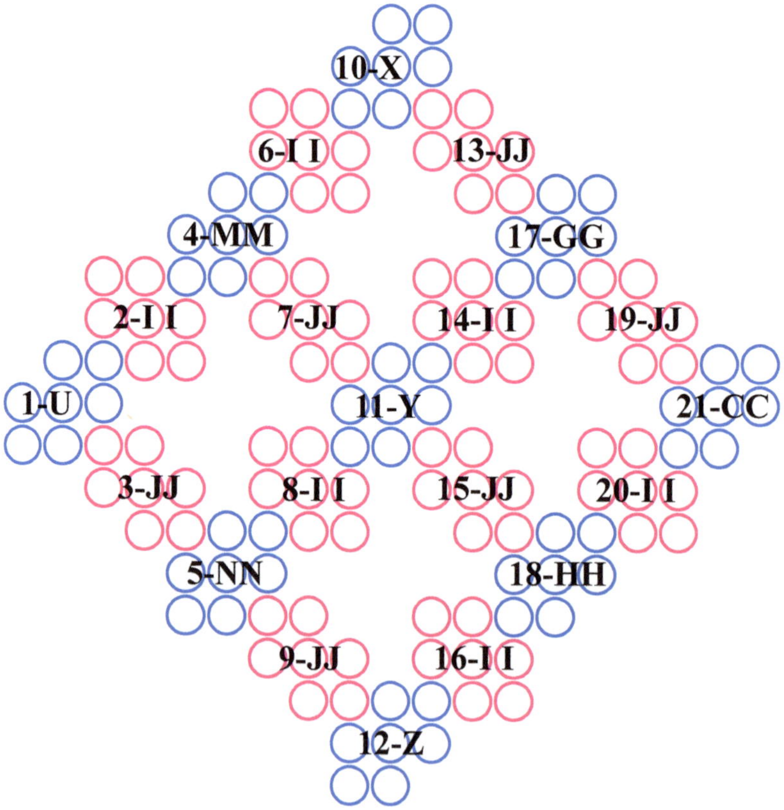

34

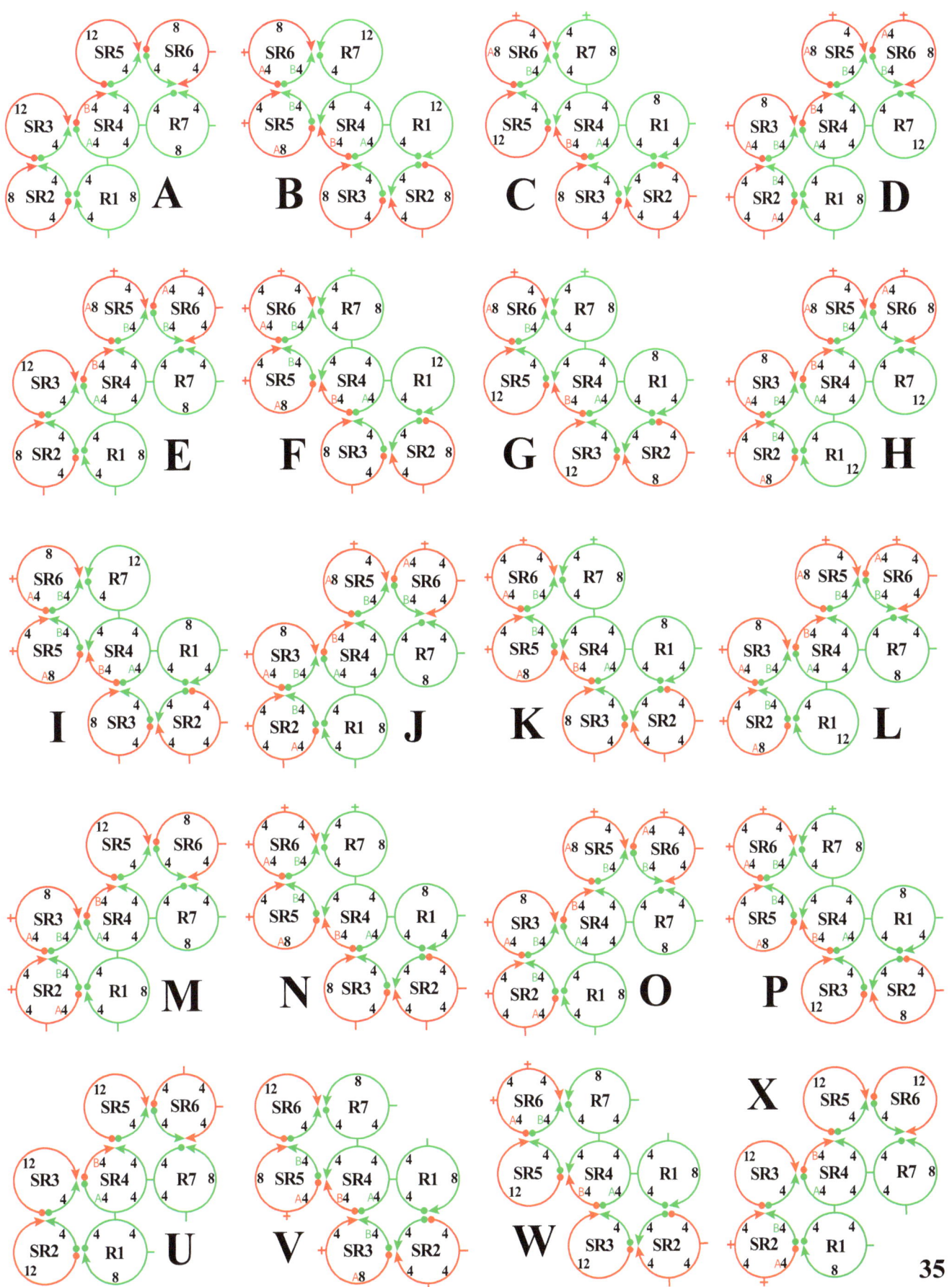

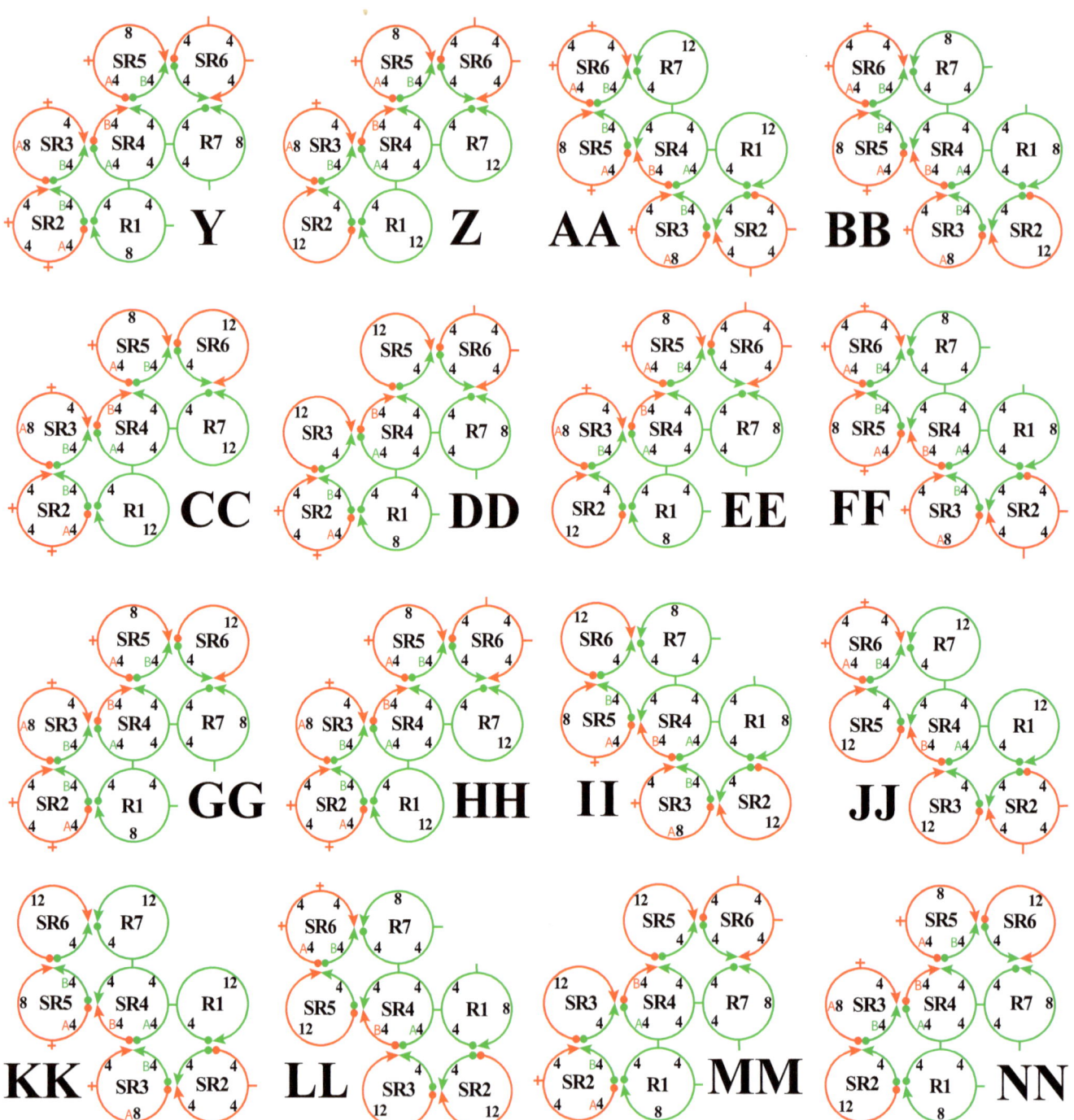

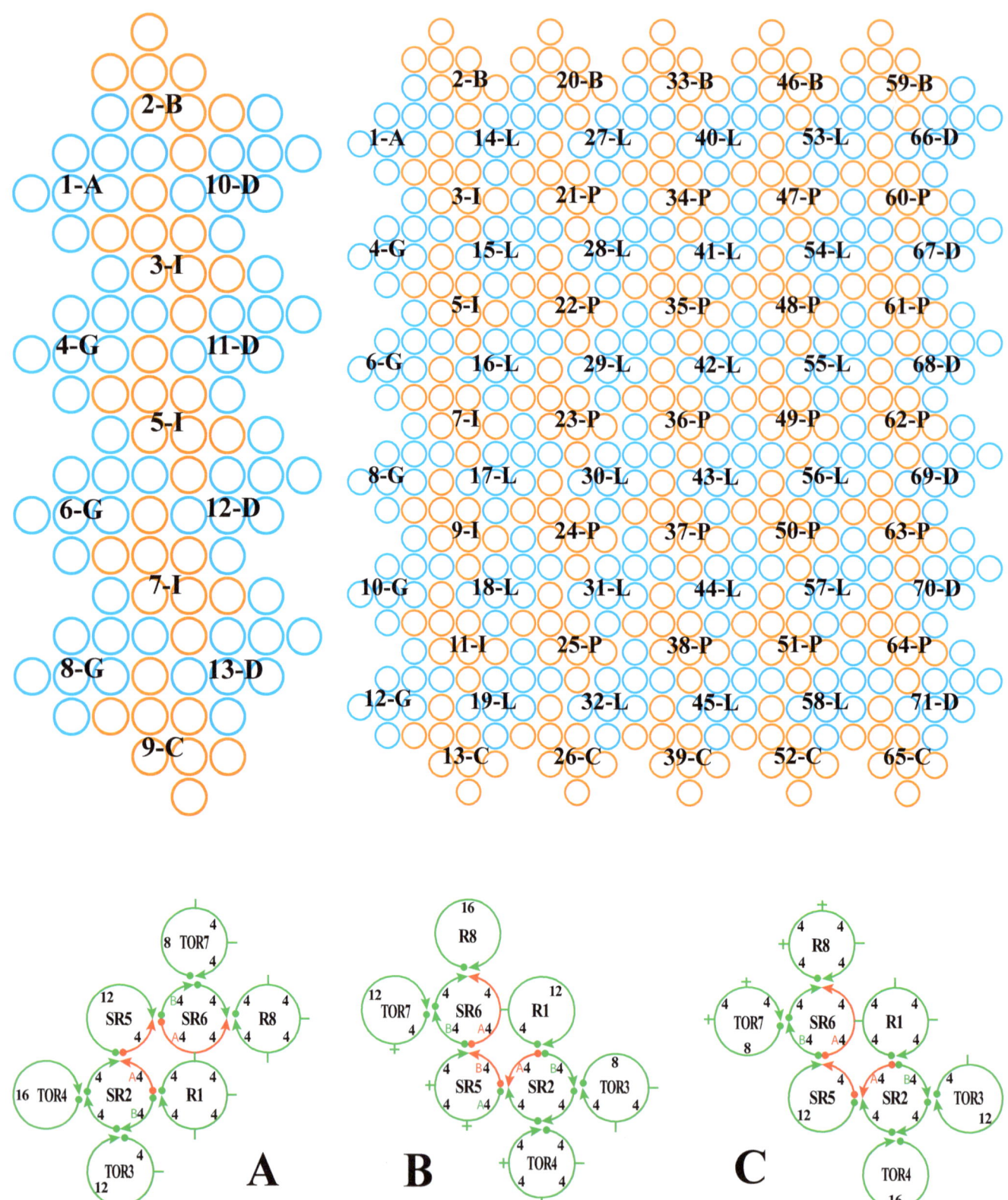

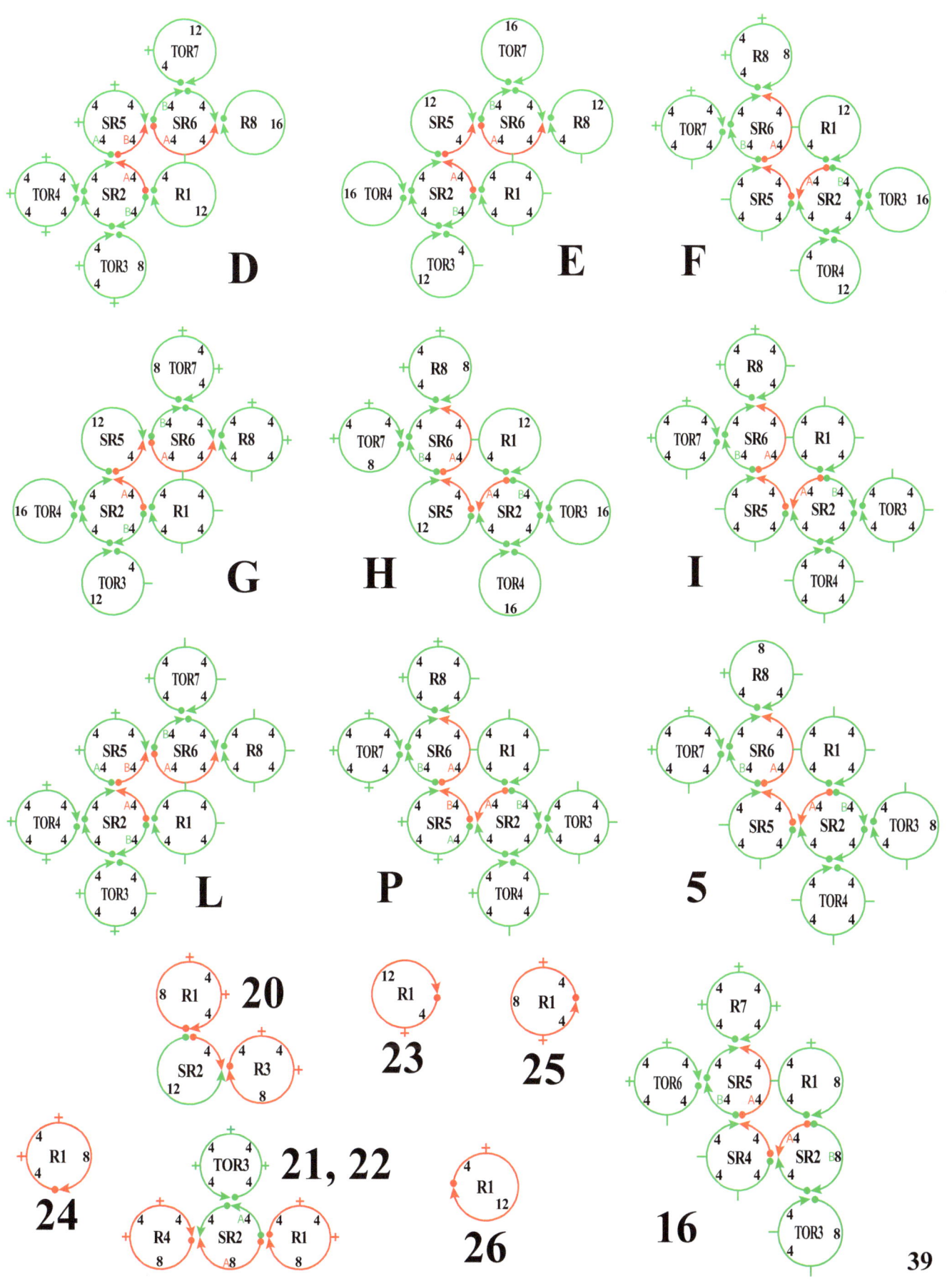

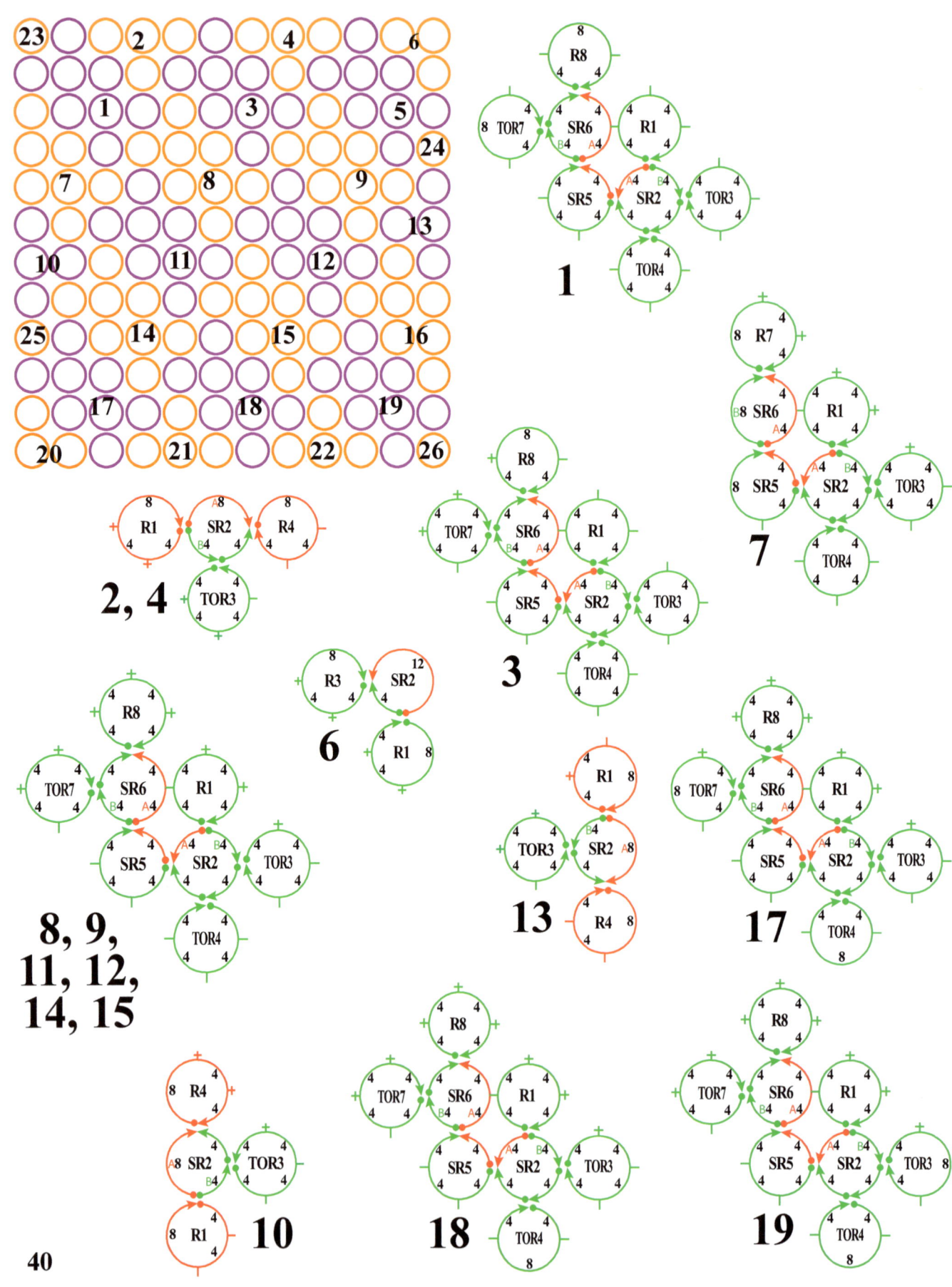

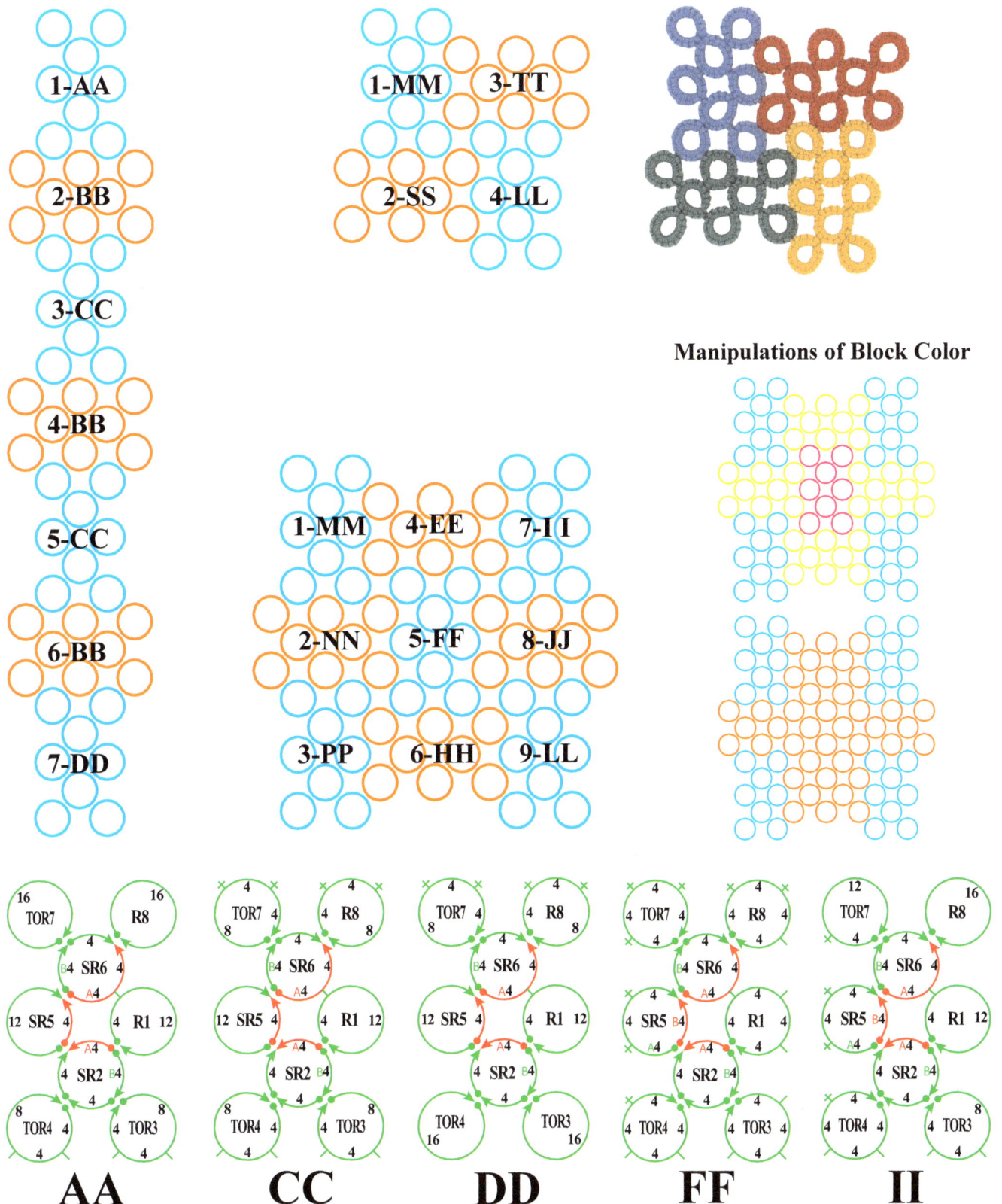

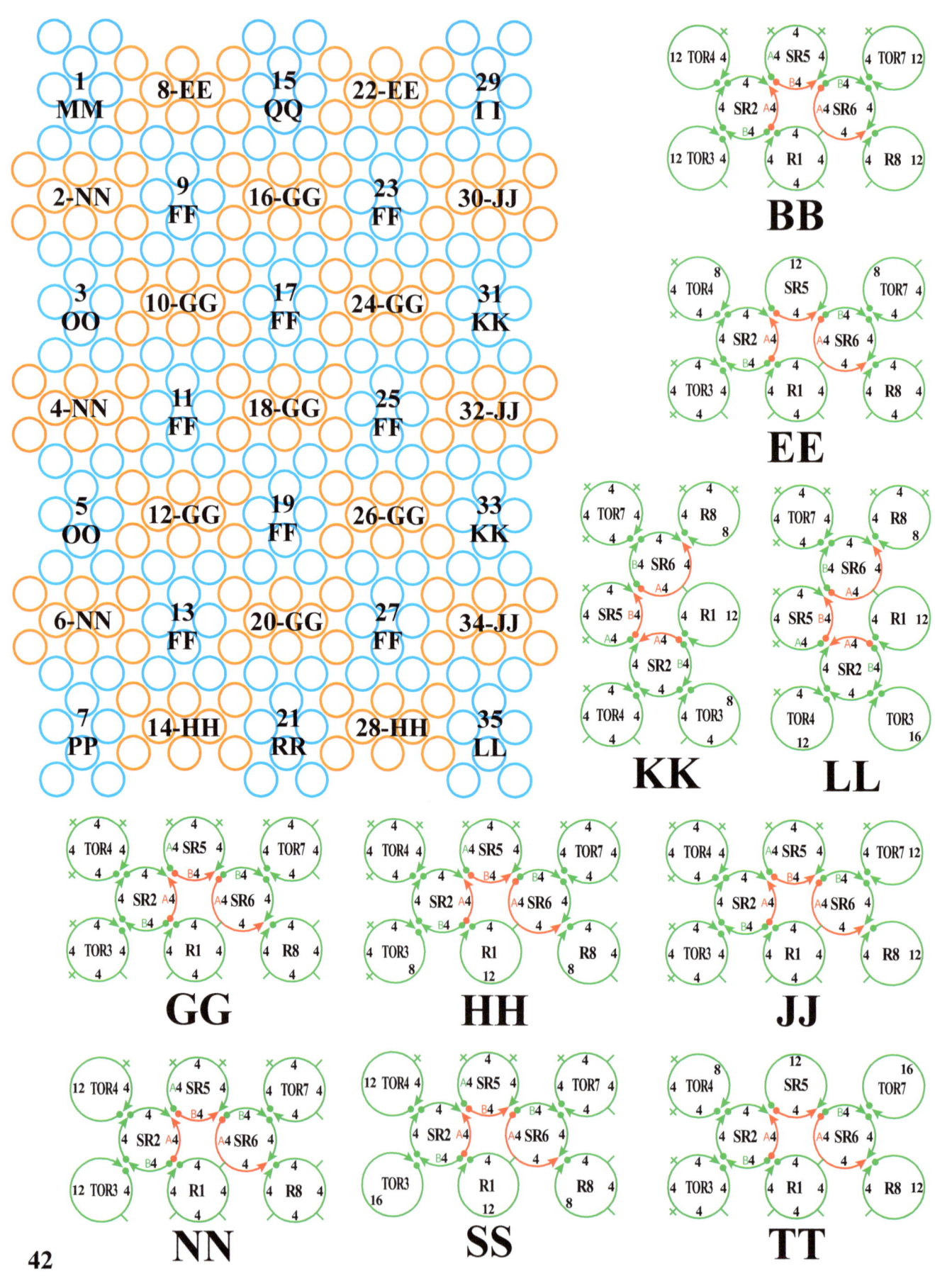

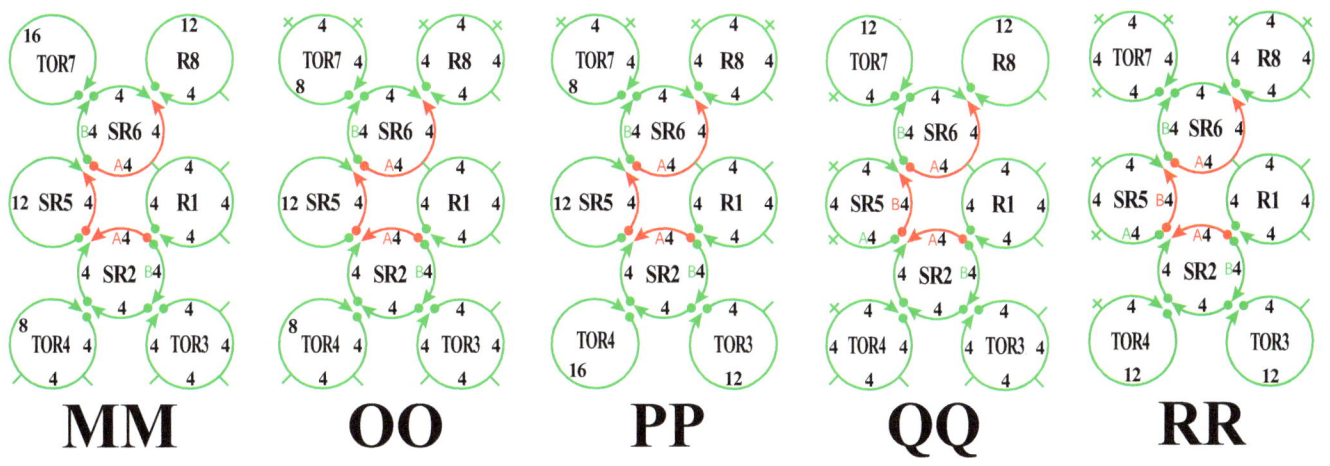

Manipulations of Block Color

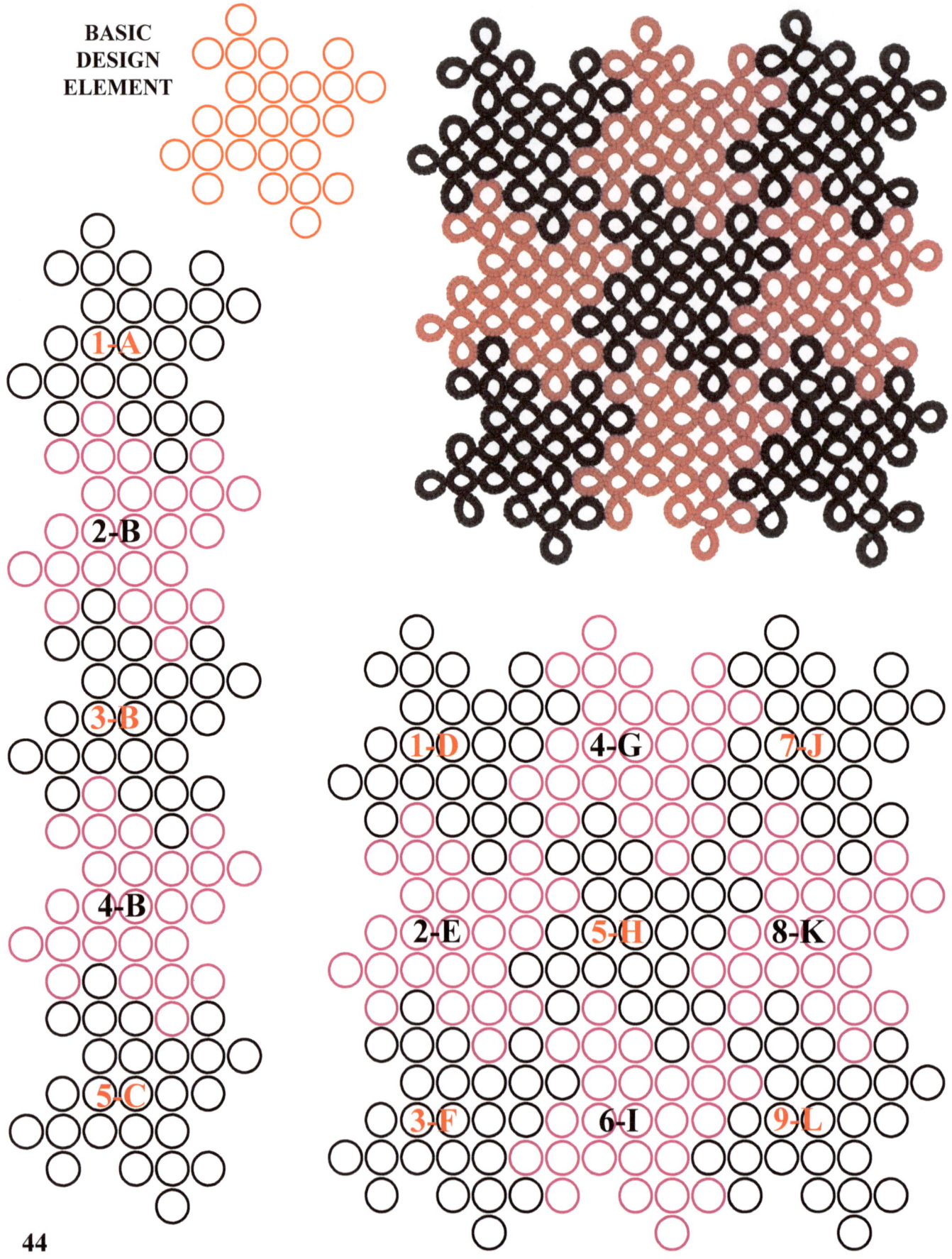

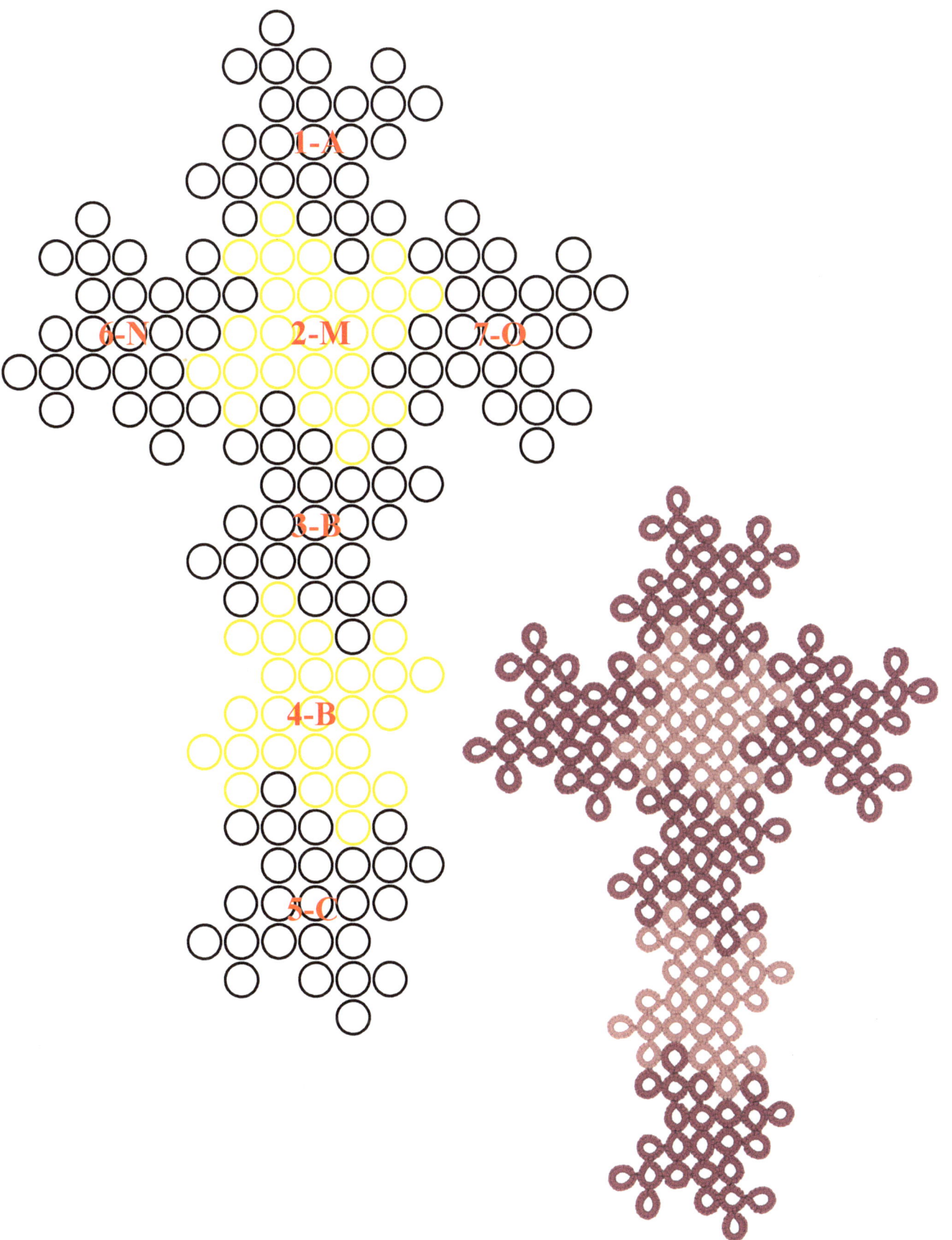

45

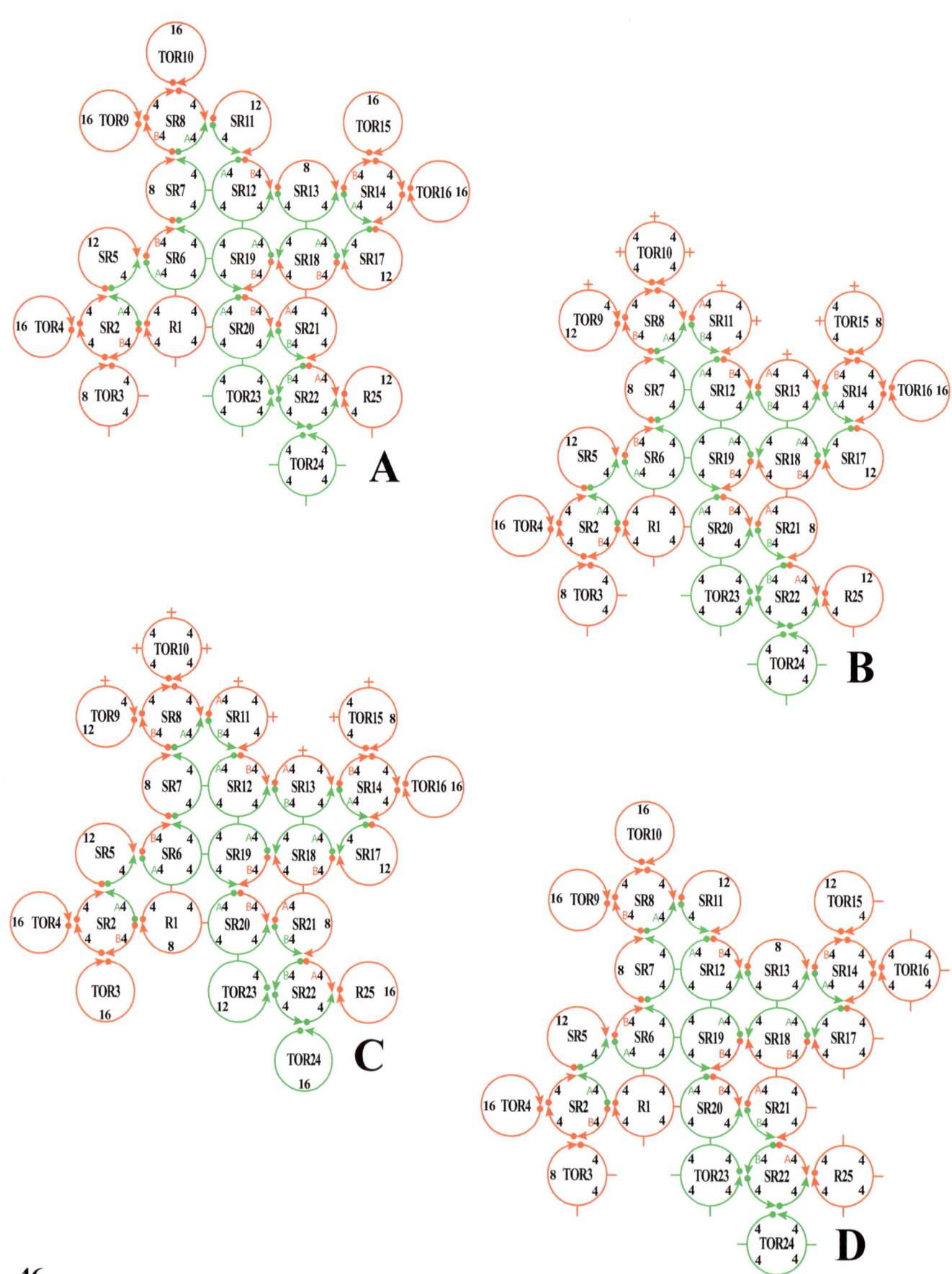

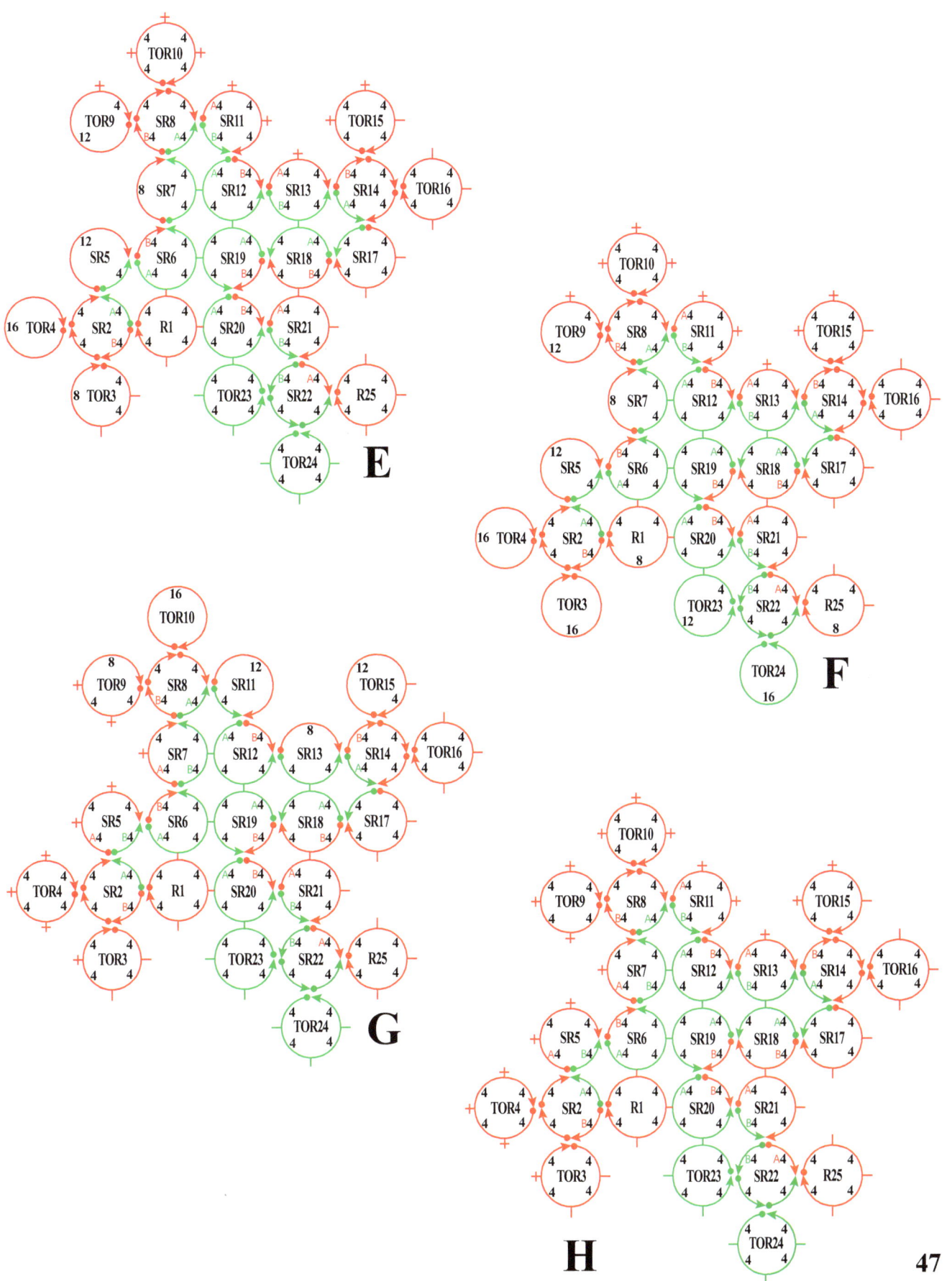

48

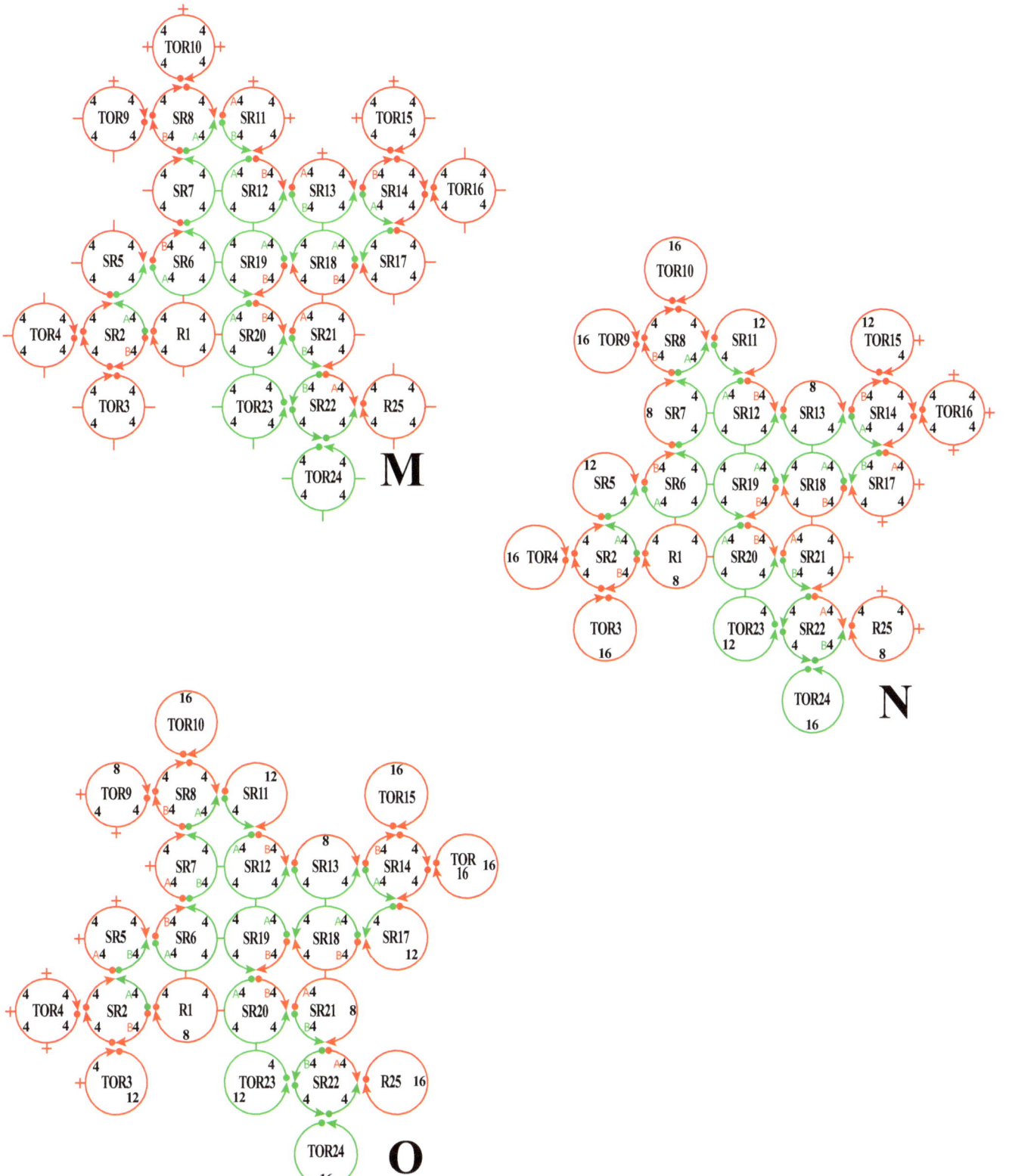

BASIC DESIGN ELEMENTS

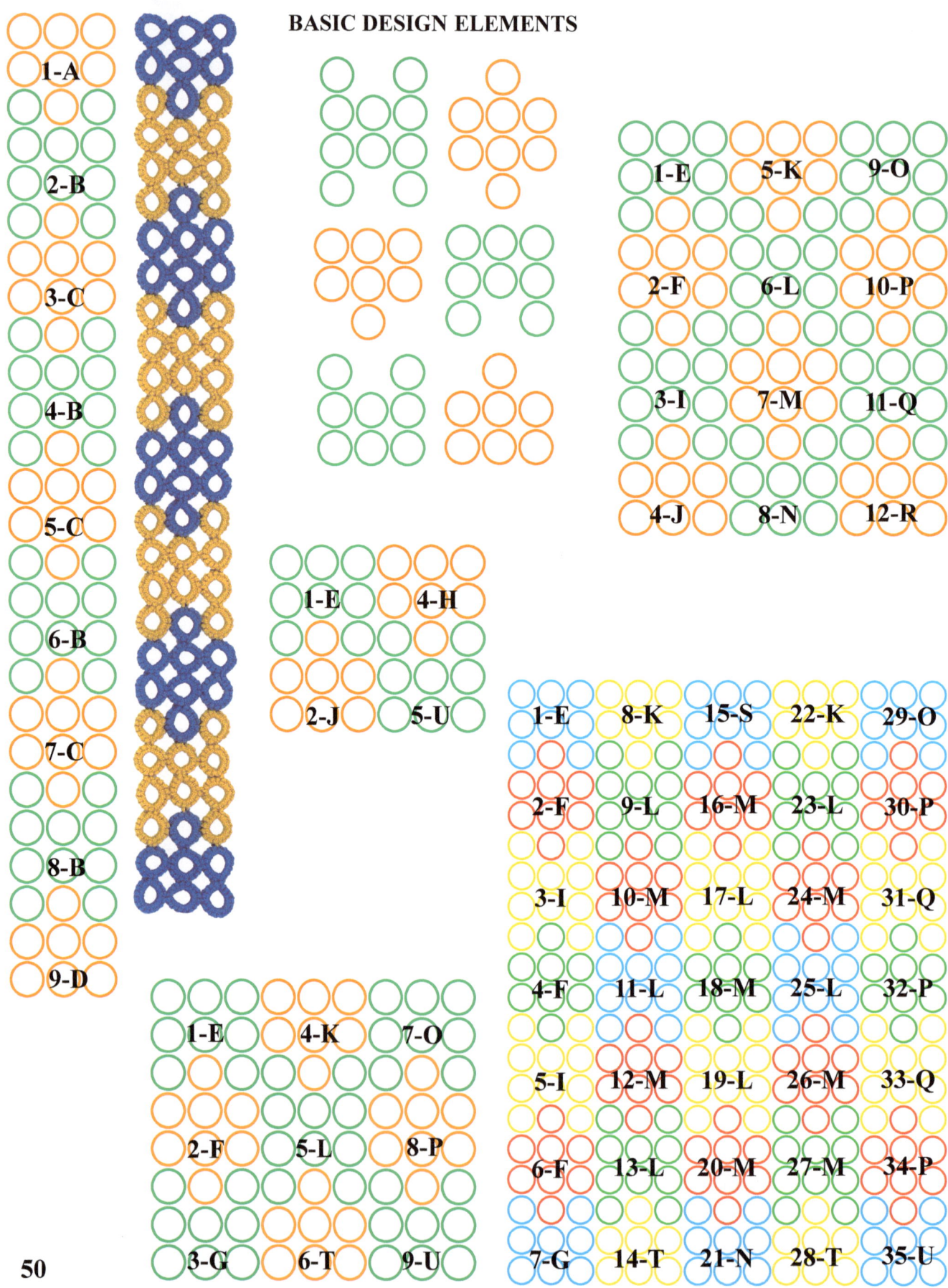

50

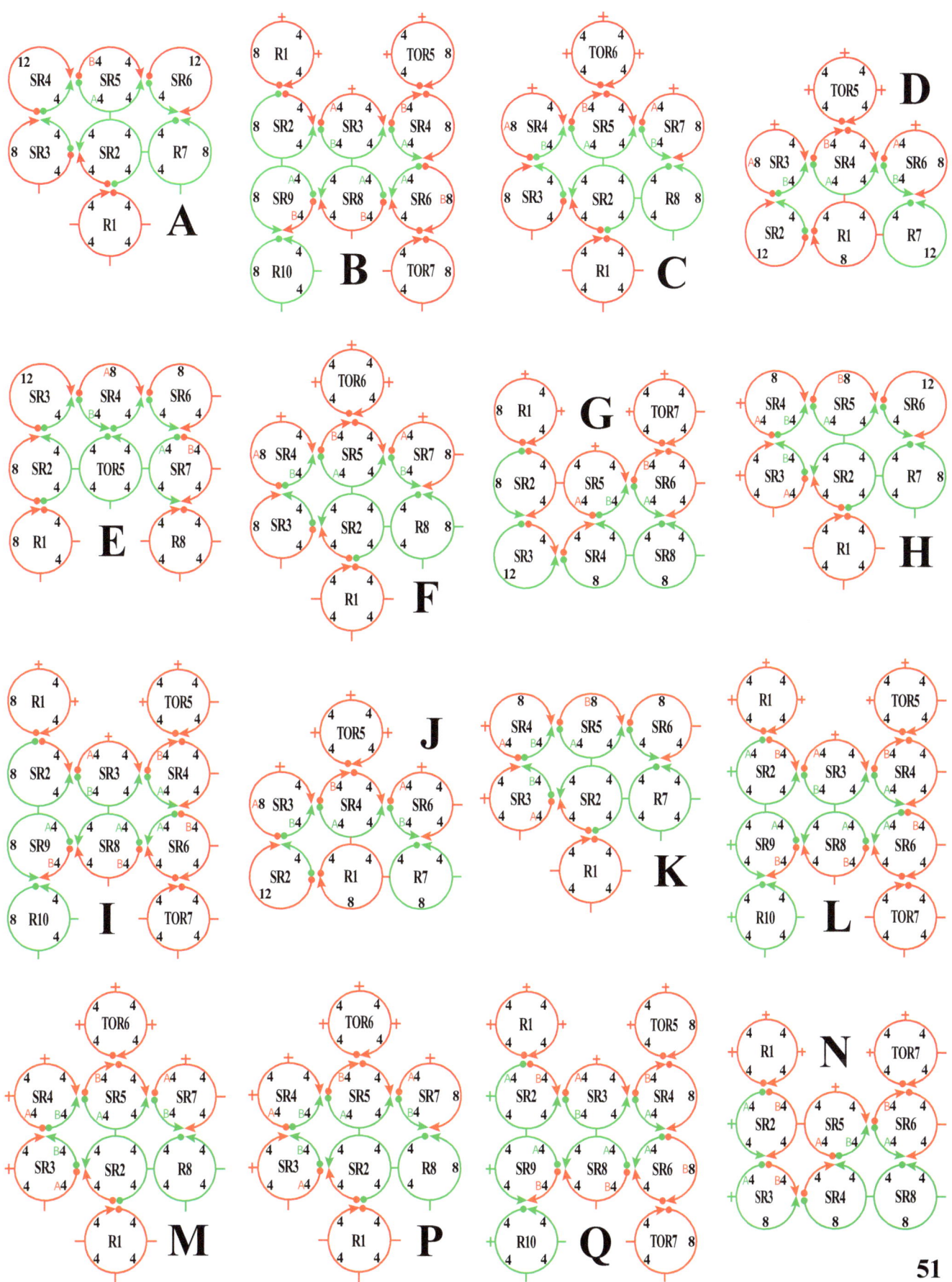

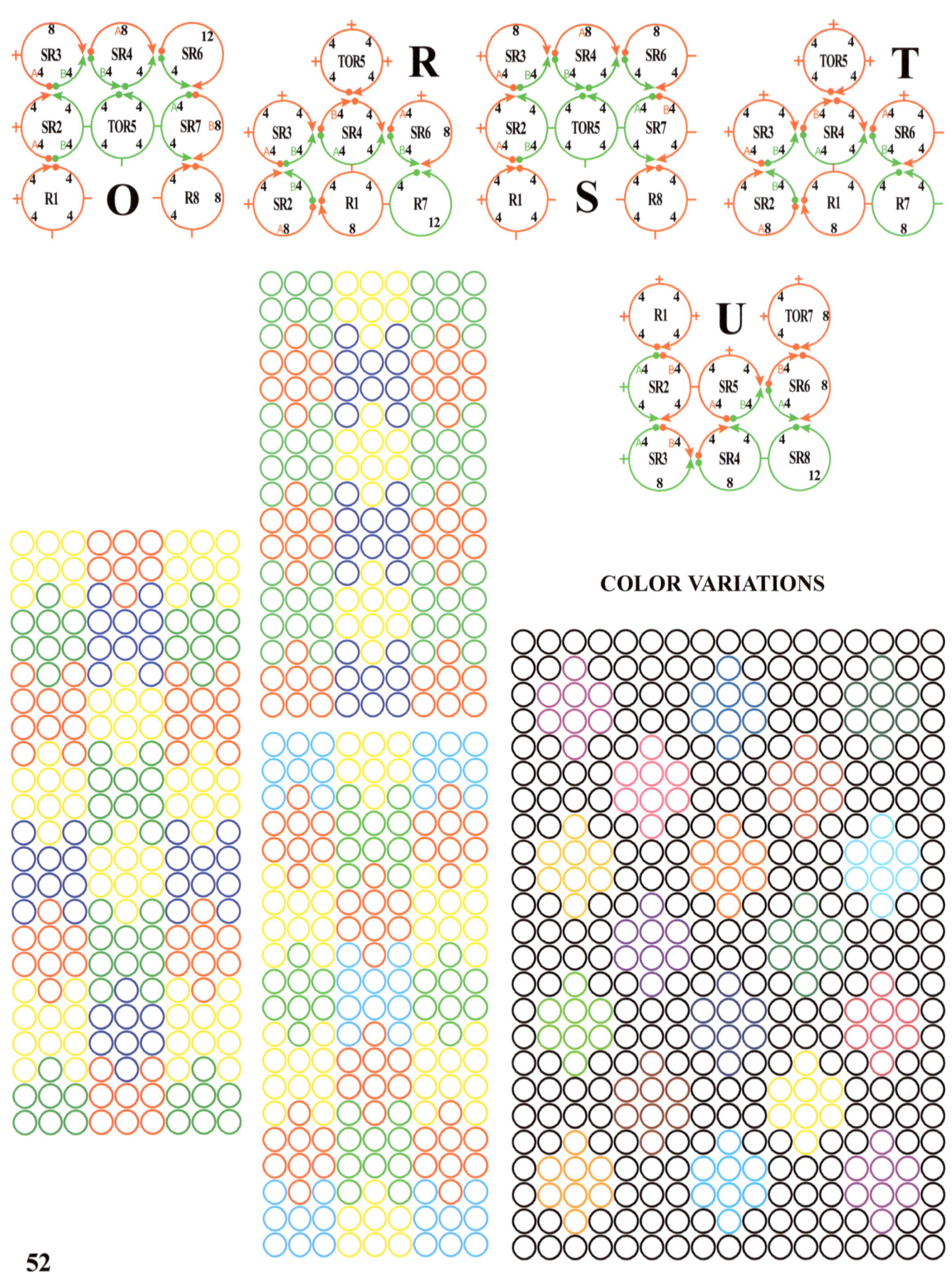

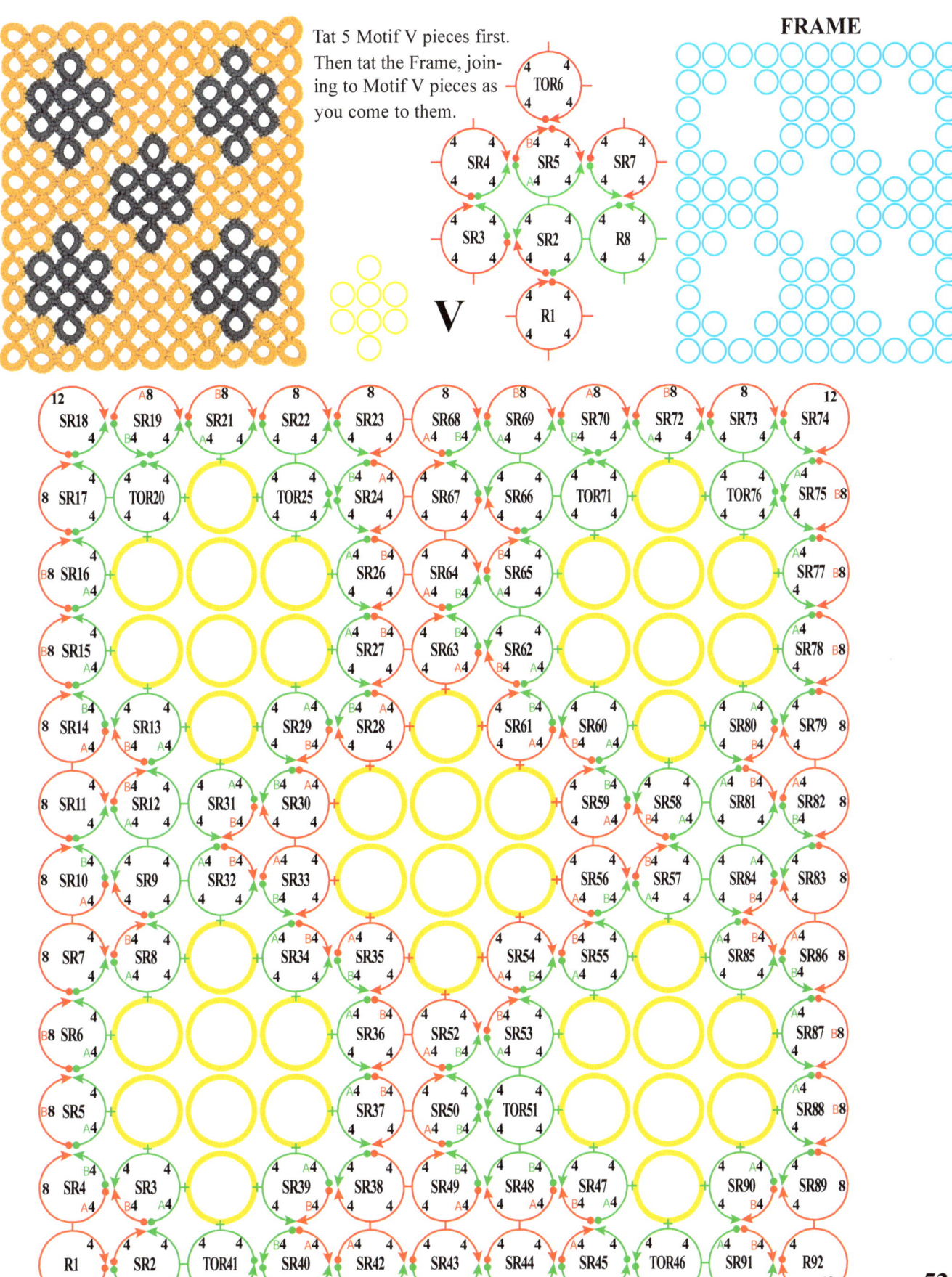

Tat the inner 9 motifs (1-V to 9-M) first. Then tat the Frame, joining to inner motif as you come to them.

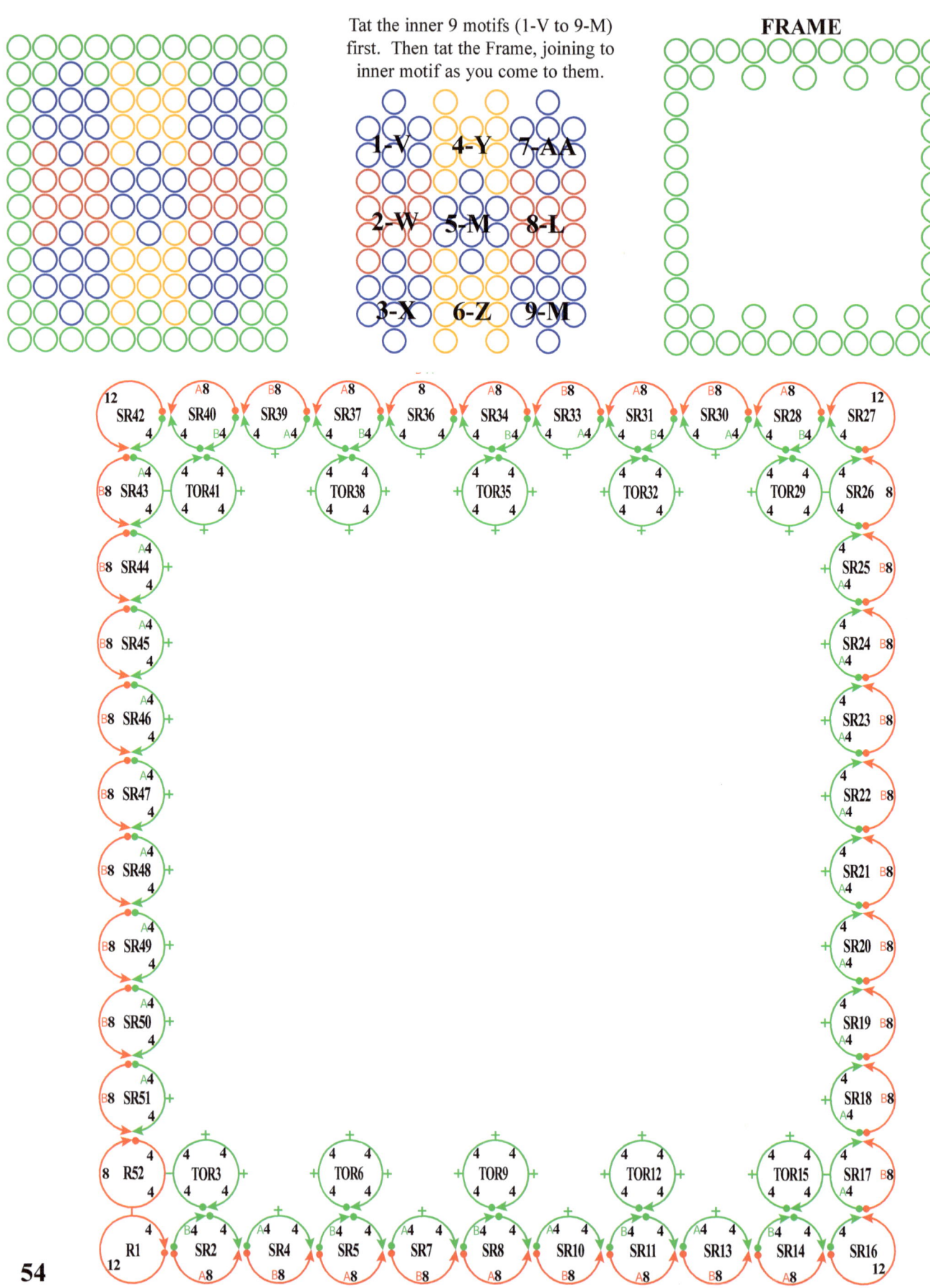

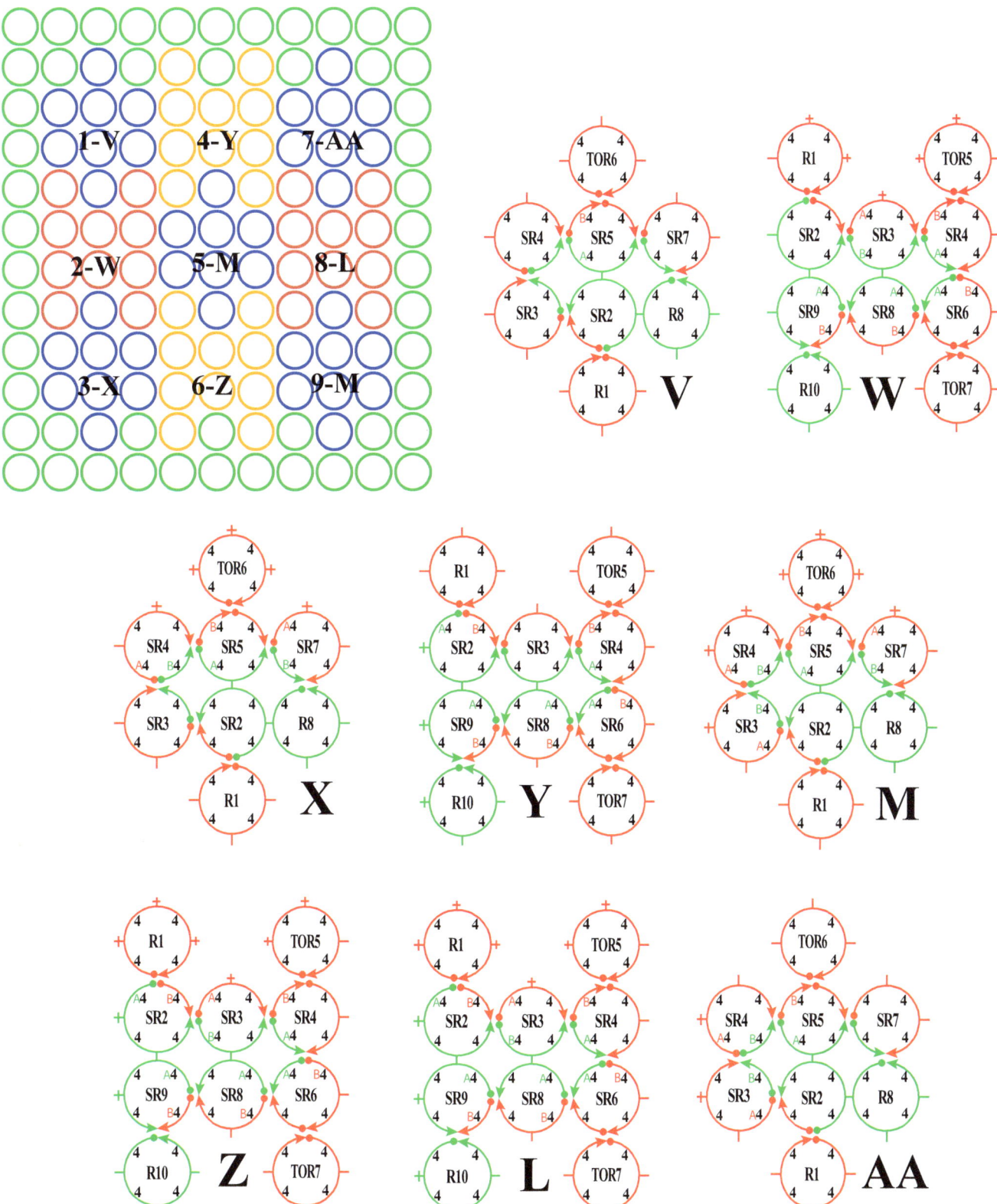

Split Ring Tatting (SRT) & Take/Thrown-Off Rings (TOR's) using Needle Tatting Technique

This instruction guide was created when a needle tatter posed the question whether the patterns in my *Fun with Split Ring Tatting* book could be used in Needle Tatting Technique (NTT).

My first knee-jerk response was 'Yes, everything that can be tatted via Shuttle Tatting Technique **can** be created in Needle Tatting Technique'. However, after that initial thought, I realized that many of my designs have Take/Thrown-Off Rings (TOR's) associated with them. So I had to take a closer look at the techniques.

I have written my own 'Introduction to Needle Tatting' book that I used in my classes teaching nationally at needlework shows. & have used Split Ring Tatting Technique in some of those classes. But even so, I consider myself a 'dabbler' in Needle Tatting Technique in that I am a long-time Shuttle Tatter.

I have created this instruction guide to demonstrate how to
- A. Create Split Rings using Needle Tatting Technique
- B. Create Take-Off (aka Thrown-Off) Rings using Needle Tatting Technique

<u>Split Ring Tatting requires two thread sources</u>.
>In Shuttle Tatting Tecnique, this is supplied by using two separate thread source, usually wound onto 2 separate shuttles.
>
>In Needle Tatting Technique, the working technique is similar to tatting a pattern that has both rings and chains, requiring two thread sources. One thread source will be the 'Auxilliary' thread and the other will be the 'Core' thread.

Needle Tatting Terminology

The *Auxilliary Thread* is the portion/segment of thread that is closest to the needle tip. It is sometimes used attached to the ball of thread.

The *Core Thread* is what is closest to the needle eye and is usually threaded through the needle's eye.

In *Fun with Split Ring Tatting* illustrated patterns, two different colors (red & green) are used to distinquish between the two thread sources.

When Split Ring Tatting using Needle Tatting Technique:
>-The red portion is tatted with the Auxilliary Thread source.
>-The green portion is tatted with the Core Thread.

The colored letters (red/green, A/B) in *Fun with Split Ring Tatting* and *MORE Fun with Split Ring Tatting* illustrated patterns do not mean anything to Needle Tatters. They exist to give direction to Shuttle Tatting Technique only.

Shuttle Tatting Technique has more innate construction constraints than Needle Tatting Technique. The colored numbers tell the shuttle tatter which thread source to use and in what order to tat the various portions of the split ring. This is due to the fact in Shuttle Tatting Technique:
>--Joins are more easily done on the first portion of the split ring--joining on the second portion requires the use of Split Ring Join Technique which is more combersome to use.
>--Take-Off Rings can only be done on the second portion of the split ring without the use of a third thread source.

This six-ring pattern will be used to demonstrate
How to create Split Rings via Needle Tatting Technique---SR2
How to create Take-Off Rings from Split Rings via Needle Tatting Technique---SR3/TOR4/TOR5.

It is assumed that the tatter is familiar with basic Needle Tatting Technique.

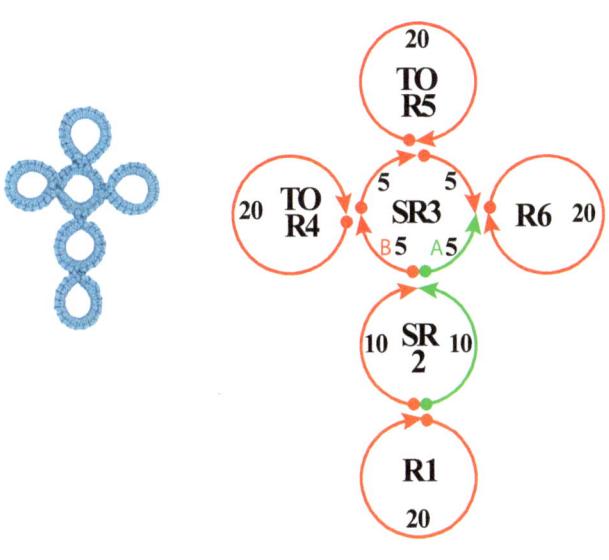

To start Ring 1: Thread the needle with thread that is still connected to the ball at this stage. This is the same way that you would start a traditional ring/chain pattern. Use as much thread 'as you can stand to work with' on the right side of the work that connects to the needle eye. **ILLUS A**

ILLUS B shows one double stitch (DS) made

Using the Auxilliary Thread, tat 20 DS's **ILLUS C**

Close Ring 1 by pushing the DS's *(in the direction of the dotted line in ILLUS C)* over the eye of the needle. Capture the stitches into a ring by inserting the needle through the ring of core thread.

ILLUS D shows R1 completed.

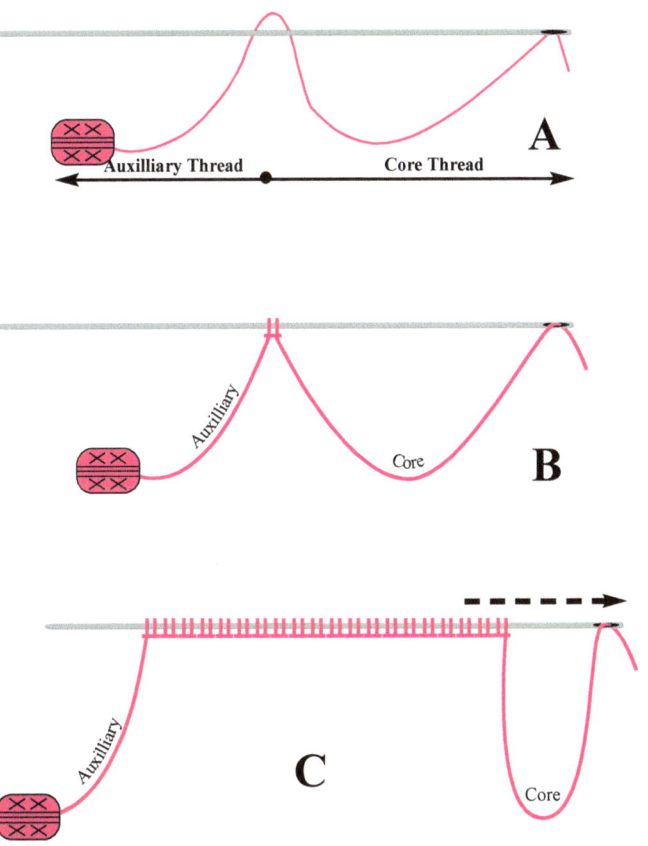

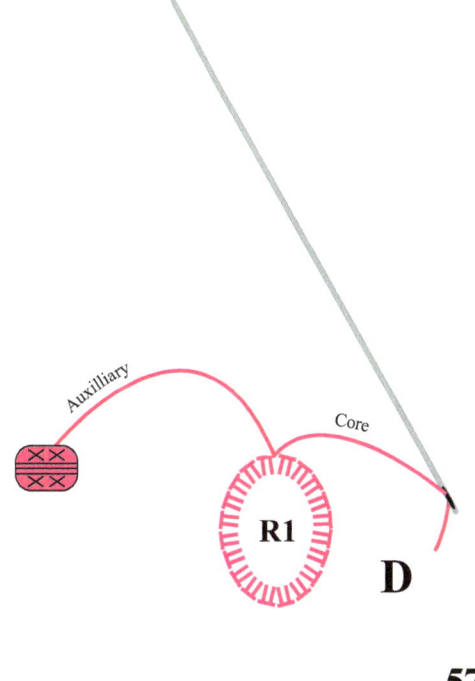

57

The following instructions and illustrations (E through K) will guide you in how to tat a basic Split Ring (SR2) in Needle Tatting Technique

Using the Auxilliary Thread, tat 10 double stitches. **ILLUS E**

Turn or Flip Work (as if you were turning the page of a book). **ILLUS F**

Take the Core Thread out of the needle eye. **ILLUS G**

Using the Core Thread, tat 10 double stitches. *Ignore the needle eye--it may be slightly bigger diameter than the needle shaft. Form/tension the stitches on the constant-diameter needle shaft.* **ILLUS H**

Turn or Flip work again. **ILLUS I**

Thread the Core Thread into the needle eye. **ILLUS J**

Close this Split ring as you would a regular ring by pushing the stitches off the needle *(in the direction of the dotted line in ILLUS J)* over the eye of the needle. Capture the stitches into a ring by inserting the needle through the ring of core thread.

ILLUS K shows SR2 completed

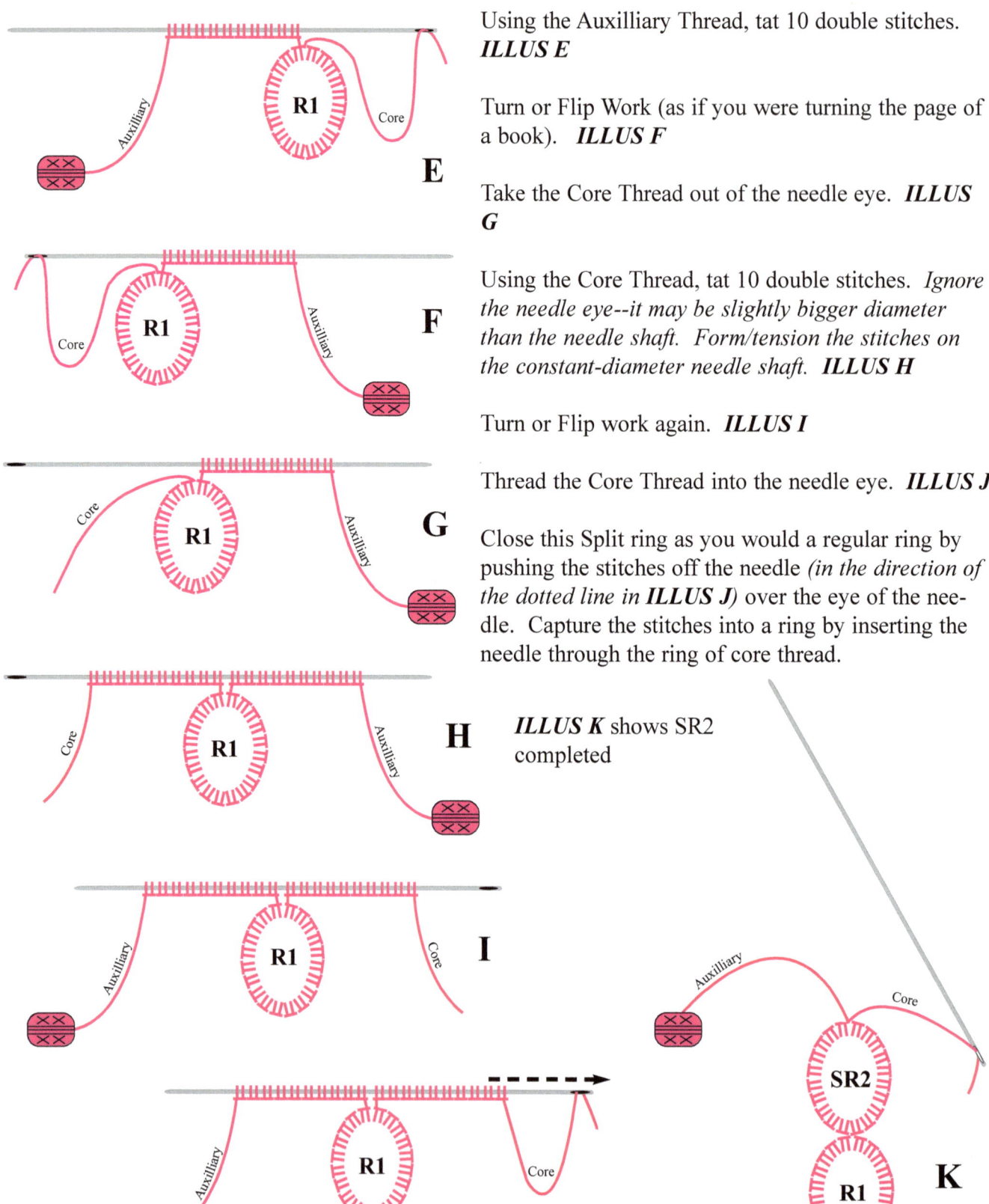

The following instructions and illustrations (L through DD) will guide you in how to tat a Split Ring (SR3) and two Take-Off Rings (TOR4 & TOR5).

To tat the Take-Off Rings you will need a second tatting needle.

These three rings are tatted as a unit in the following way:

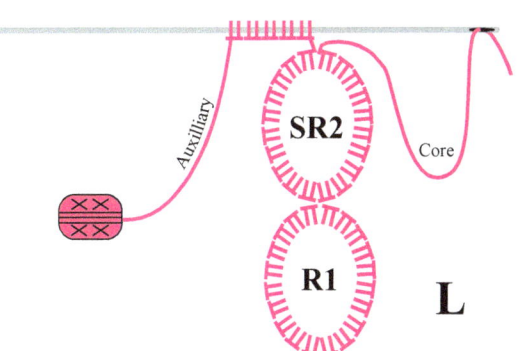

Using Auxilliary Thread, tat 5 double stitches. **ILLUS L**

Turn the work 90 degress, clock-wise, needle tip pointing up. **ILLUS M**

Bring the second needle up to the last double stitch made. **ILLUS N**

To create TOR4: use Auxilliary Thread to tat 20 double stitches on the second needle. **ILLUS O & P**

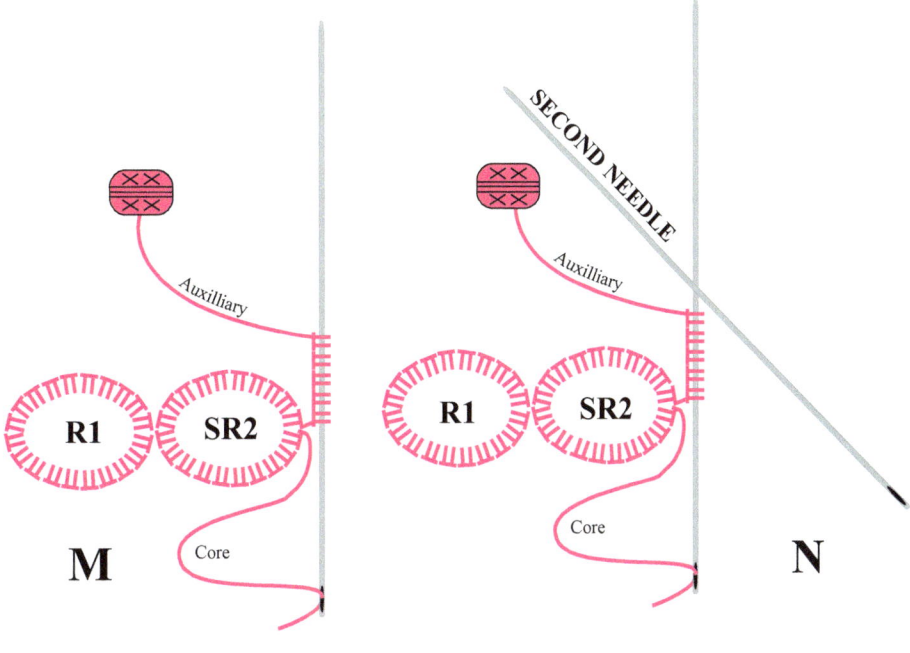

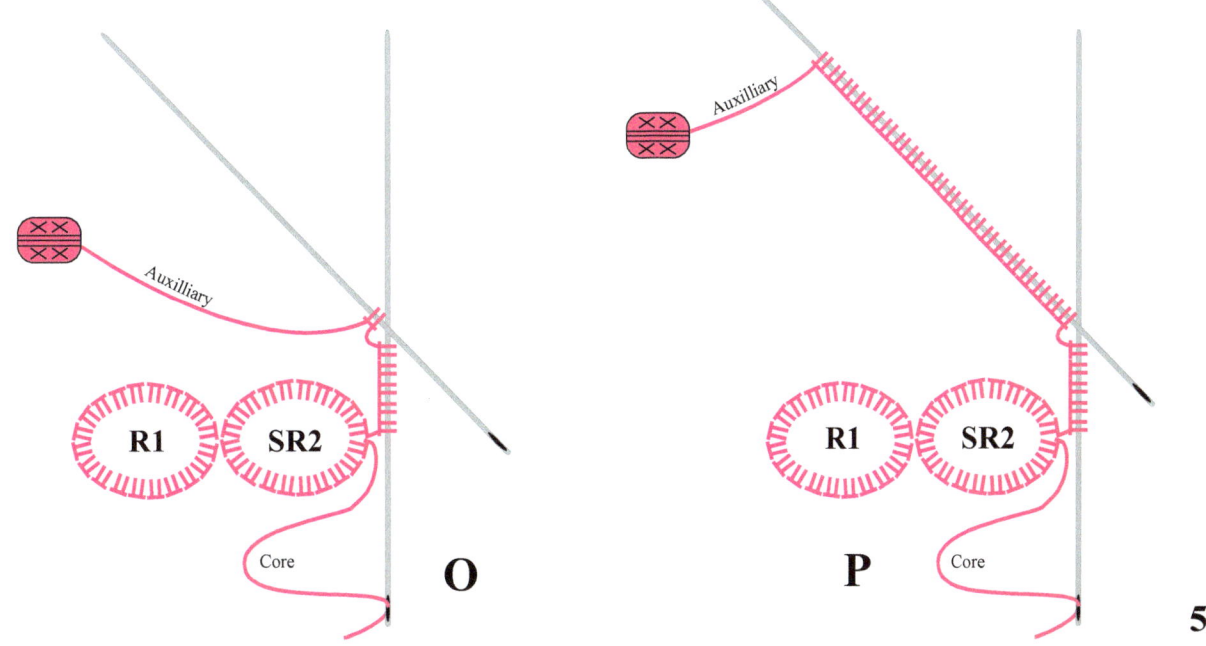

Up to this point, the Auxilliary Thread could be used still attached to the original ball of thread.

Now the Auxilliary Thread needs to be cut away from the ball for the next step. Measure off as much thread 'as you can stand to work with'.

Thread this Auxilliary Thread end into the second needle eye. **ILLUS Q**

Close TOR4 by pushing the stitches off the second needle *(in the direction of the dotted line in **ILLUS Q**)*, over the needle eye. The double stitches will be automatically formed into a ring. **ILLUS R**

Unthread Auxilliary Thread from the second needle. *(You are now done using the second needle for a while.)*

Turn work 90 degrees counterclockwise, needle tip pointing to left. **ILLUS S**

Using Auxilliary Thread make 5 double stitches. **ILLUS T** *(These are the 5 DS's of SR3 between TOR4 & TOR5)*

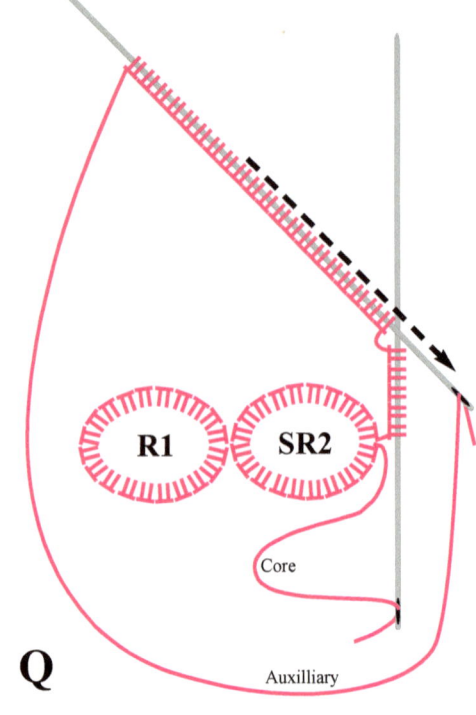

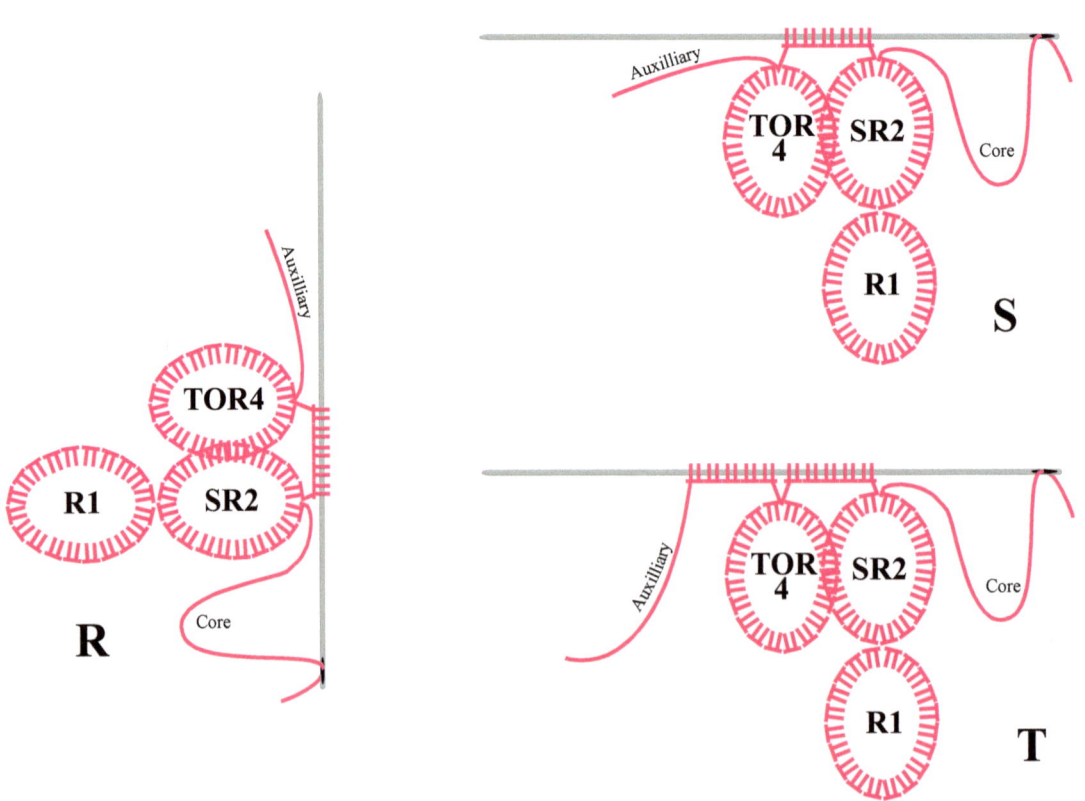

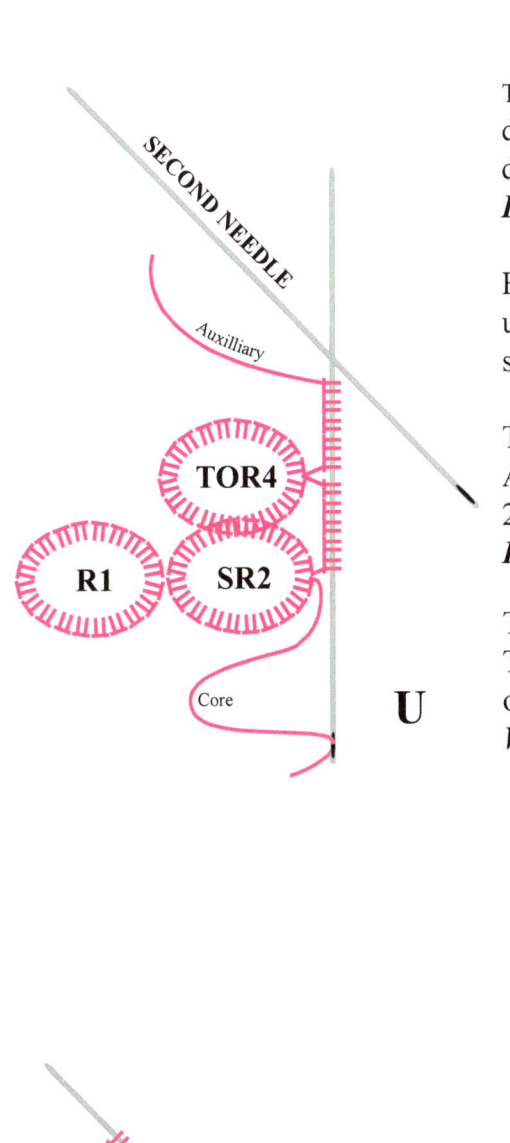

Turn the work 90 degress clock-wise, needle tip pointing up. ***ILLUS U***

Bring the second needle up to the last double stitch made. ***ILLUS U***

To create TOR5: use Auxilliary Thread to tat 20 double stitches. ***ILLUS V***

Thread Auxilliary Thread end into the second needle eye. ***ILLUS W***

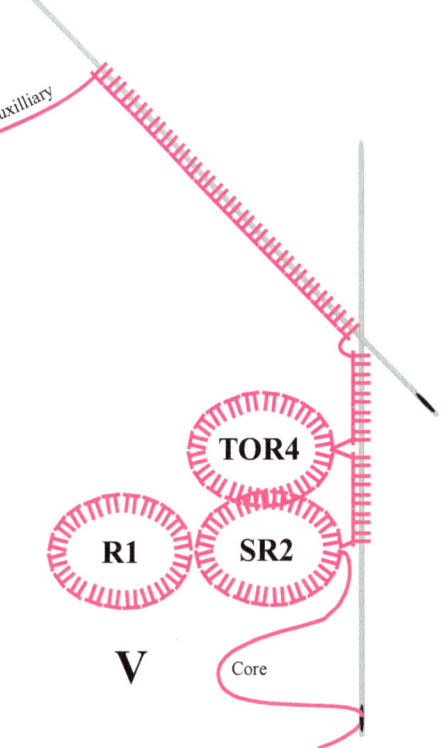

Close TOR5 by pushing the stitches off the second needle *(in the direction of the dotted line in **ILLUS W**)*, over the needle eye. The double stitches will be automatically formed into a ring. ***ILLUS X***

Unthread Auxilliary Thread from the second needle. *(You are now done using the second needle.)*

Turn work 90 degrees counterclockwise, needle tip facing to the left. ***ILLUS Y***

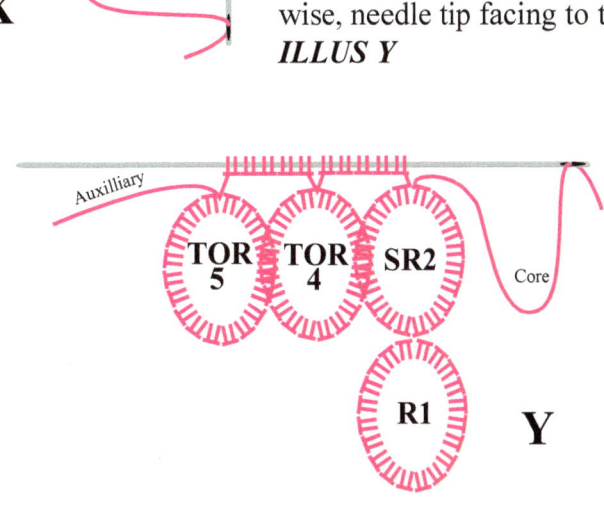

We are still working on the SR3/TOR4/TOR5 unit.

Using the Auxilliary Thread tat 5 double stitches. *(These are the last set of 5 DS's of SR3, between TOR5 and R6)* **ILLUS Z**

Turn/Flip the work (as if you were turning a page in a book). **ILLUS AA**

Unthread the Core Thread from the needle eye. **ILLUS BB**

Using the Core Thread tat 5 double stitches. *Ignore the needle eye--it may be slightly bigger diameter than the needle shaft. Form/tension the stitches on the constant-diameter needle shaft.* **ILLUS CC**

Turn/Flip the work (as if you were turning a page in a book). **ILLUS DD**

Thread the Core Thread through the needle eye. **ILLUS EE**

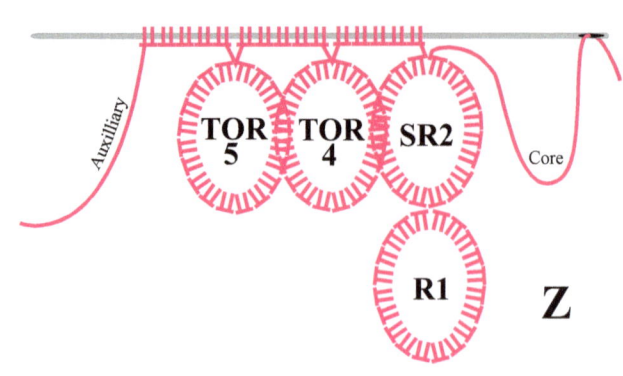

Z

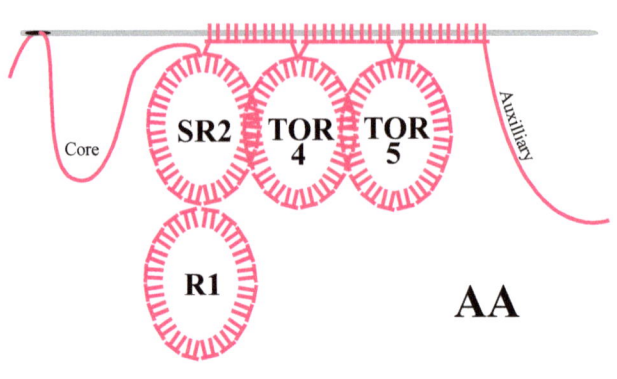

AA

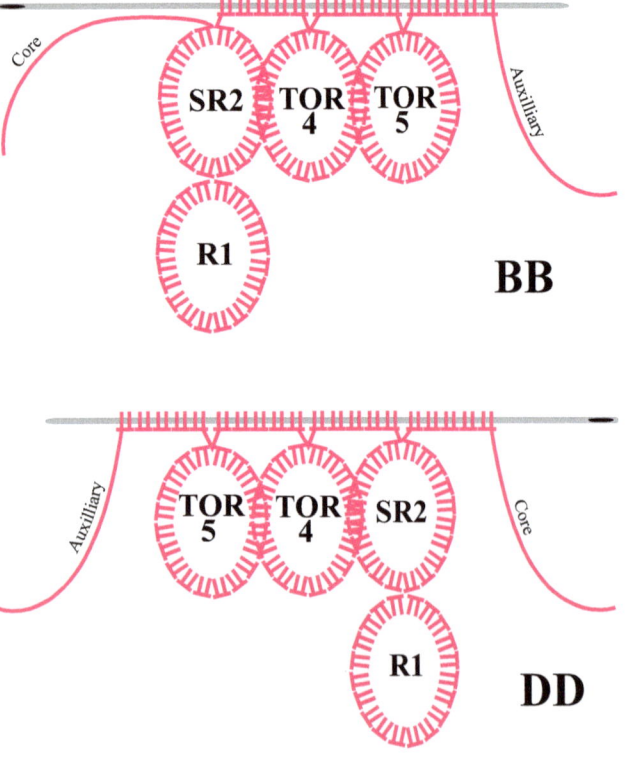

BB

DD

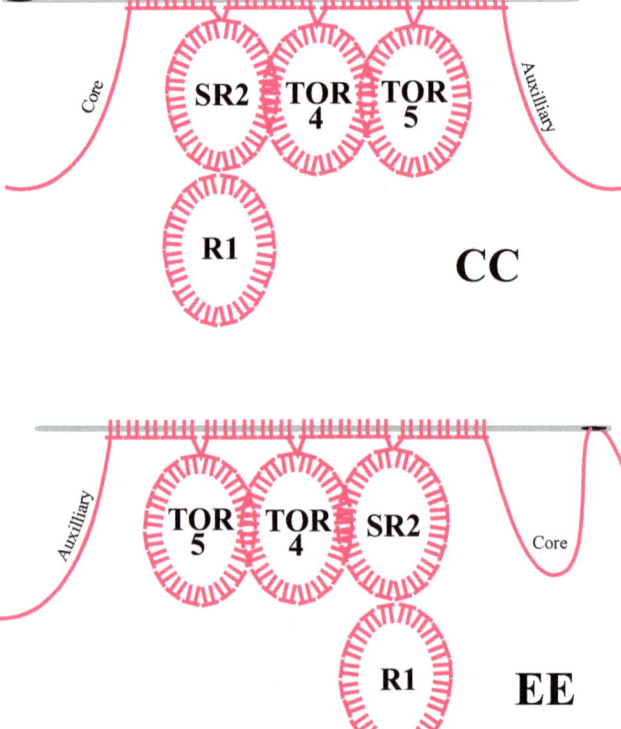

CC

EE

Close this Split Ring (SR3) as you would a regular ring by pushing the stitches off the needle, over the needle eye. Capture the stitches into a ring by inserting the needle through the ring of core thread. **ILLUS FF**

(You have just completed the SR3/TOR4/TOR5 unit).

Create R6 by using Auxilliary Thread to tat 20 double stitches. **ILLUS GG**

Close R6 as you would a regular ring by pushing the stitches off the needle *(in the direction of the dotted line in ILLUS GG)*, over the needle eye. Capture the stitches into a ring by inserting the needle through the ring of core thread.

ILLUS HH shows the completed piece.

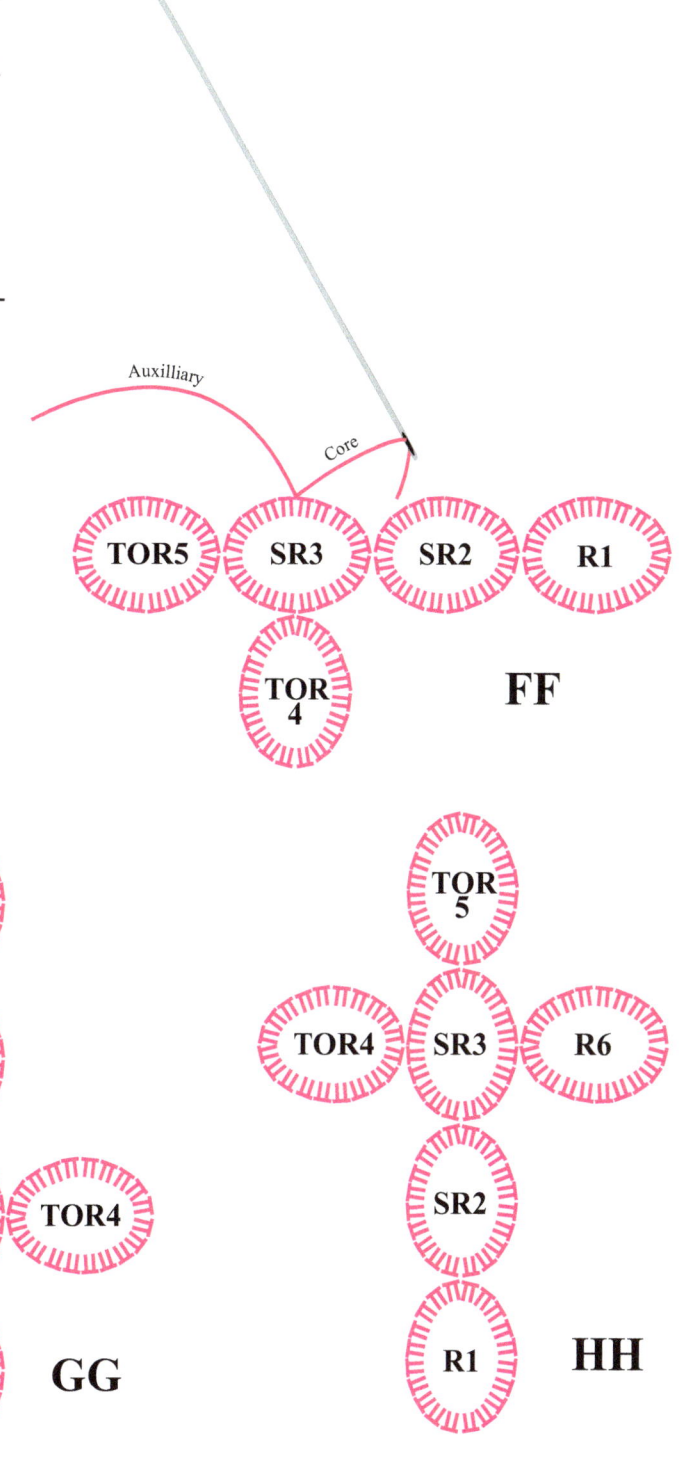

www.ingramcontent.com/pod-product-compliance
Lightning Source LLC
Chambersburg PA
CBHW042026150426
43198CB00002B/78